PRAISE FOR

ESCAPE to the TATRAS
A BOY, A WAR AND A LIFE INTERRUPTED

"Oscar Sladek writes, 'I was too young' - too young to be confronted with the horrors of the Holocaust and the brutal costs of escape. But, as this extraordinary account shows, young Oscar already had an unfailing eye for the perennial truths of human courage, compassion, and the power of faith. He was not too young to stand upright in the center of a rare heroism, with his beloved Anyu and Apu, accumulating experience that would shape the moral imagination that makes this book a masterpiece of love and survival."

- JAMES CARROLL
Winner of the National Book Award, *An American Requiem*
Winner of the National Jewish Book Award, *Constantine's Sword*

"Oscar Sladek's *Escape to the Tatras* is the moving and suspenseful story of a child's survival against daunting and ever worsening, odds. Written in straightforward language, and in terms designed to educate those less familiar with Jewish culture and the history of the Holocaust, it is both a powerful testament to a family's determination to save themselves and a vivid illustration of where ethnic and religious hatred can lead if left unchecked. As time marches on, and as eyewitness survivors of the Shoah grow fewer and fewer, books such as this are invaluable reminders of humanity's obligation to work to ensure that such horrors are never repeated; that children are free to experience their childhoods free of the desperation and fear that the author was forced to endure. *Escape to the Tatras*, a meaningful educational resource accessible to both educators and students, allows readers to celebrate Sladek's ultimate survival while being reminded of this ever important message."

- CHRIS LEPPEK
Intermountain Jewish News (Denver)
Author of *Apollonia* and *The Surrogate Assassin*

"Oscar Sladek's captivating memoir written through the lens of a nine-year-old boy gives us unique insight into the role children played during the Holocaust. He teaches us about the power of the human spirit, how hope and optimism can carry you through the most harrowing times, and that taking extreme risks are worth it when fighting for what's right."

- **BETH KEAN**
Chief Executive Officer
Holocaust Museum LA

"In writing this most touching and moving Holocuast survivor memoir, Oscar Sladek articulates, perhaps, the most profound fact of all: everyday life is lived between the extremes of good and evil, life and death. There is no more significant lesson than this, as taught by a wise man recounting the most trying recollections of his youth, and the loss of youth. We can all recall ourselves at eight, nine, ten years of age. To imagine we, ourselves, enduring the traumas accounted for in Mr. Sladek's narrative, brings the magnitude of history down to the graspable, tangible reality of his life story. The educational and experiential significance of this becomes more critical with each passing day as the rhetoric of our era, the polarization of our communities, and the efforts to place one another in opposite and extreme camps becomes ever more prevalent. Osi Sladek survived the gradual and methodological efforts of demonization. Millions upon millions of others did not. His journey through one of the darkest periods in human history, demands of us to learn, and learn anew, and to teach unrelentingly, that such horrors have and can happen again. And we have the capacity to fight against such evil."

- **RABBI JAY A. STREAR**
President & Chief Executive Officer
JEWISHcolorado

"This is the inspirational story of the childhood of Oscar Sladek. Separated from his parents, barely escaping the horrors of the Holocaust, he begins a heroic journey to find safety. Along the way he learns to appreciate many of the people he encounters and the world around him. This book is both particular in its uniqueness and yet one that has wide resonance because of its humanity. There are profound lessons for us in Oscar's story as he faces life with faith and compassion."

- AMBASSADOR AKBAR AHMED
Professor of International Relations
Ibn Khaldun Chair of Islamic Studies
American University, Washington D.C.

"*Escape to the Tatras* describes the remarkable experiences of Holocaust survivor Oscar Sladek. Even as a young boy, Osi demonstrated an empathy, courageousness, and resilience that define the man he became. In this book, he shares painful memories of the immeasurable loss of his extended family and friends, but is still able to focus on righteous people, from Judge Šolc, who provided his family with advanced notice of Nazi round ups, to the partisans, who kept the family from starving. This wonderful book, and Osi's lifelong work as a respected Jewish community leader, celebrated artist and Holocaust educator, underscore his message that we should never forget those that were lost or the wonderful allies that enabled the survival of Osi, his parents and so many others."

- SCOTT L. LEVIN
Mountain States Regional Director
Anti-Defamation League

"Told through the eyes of a child, this unique tale of suffering and survival opens up an unprecedented dimension of the Event we call the Holocaust. This testimony, moving and powerful, reveals how far the horizons of this devastation extend. *Escape to the Tatras* is written with literary art that drives home the ineffable. This is truly a unique and invaluable addition to the canon of Holocaust literature."

- DAVID PATTERSON
Hillel A. Feinberg Distinguished Chair in Holocaust Studies
Ackerman Center for Holocaust Studies, University of Texas at Dallas

"For several decades, Oscar "Osi" Sladek has addressed groups about his survival during the Holocaust. Now, we have the full story in a moving autobiographical account of his childhood. As a young boy, he made daring passages from his home in Czechoslovakia to relatives in Hungary and back again. As the Nazis closed in, his family made the courageous decision to escape to the Tatra mountains. Osi shares the remarkable stories of his family's desperate attempt to evade the Nazis and survive the war: heroism and despair, pride, fear, acts of great generosity and pitiful failures of human spirit and dignity. With extraordinary honesty and candor, he holds nothing back to give the reader an intimate feel and a personal connection to his heart-wrenching and, ultimately, inspiring experiences. We have long admired Osi for his fabulous voice and musical talent; he has touched our lives as a gifted teacher and as a community leader. Now we are privileged to learn more about the dynamic spirit at his core, a spirit that was evident even when he was a child. *Escape to the Tatras* is an important book that persons of all ages should read."

- RABBI RICK RHEINS
Senior Rabbi
Temple Sinai, Denver CO

"Osi Sladek has dedicated himself to telling his story to countless students over the years. It is a privilege to be in the room and feel transformed through the power of his words and the determination of his spirit. Now, with his story in print, students can study what triumph over adversity truly means and be inspired to make a positive difference in the world, just as Osi has done."

- PENNY NISSON
Director of Education
Mizel Museum, Denver CO

"Osi's story is triumphant on so many levels. His survival with his family, his loss of his childhood, his early entry into adulthood, and still, he maintained his faith and belief in man to rise up and fulfill his potential. Hearing this memoir in the voice of a child delivers a powerful perspective we do not often hear, sharing another side of survival."

- ANDY MALLEN
Vice President, Education & Advocacy
Hadassah L.E.A. Chapter, Colorado

"Oscar Sladek's harrowing experiences as a young boy and the trauma and devastation his family suffered during the Holocaust - as memorialized in *Escape To The Tatras* - is truly one of the most inspirational stories ever told about the human spirit and the sheer will to survive."

- DAVID PERMUT
Academy Award Nominated Producer
Hacksaw Ridge

ESCAPE to the TATRAS

A BOY, A WAR AND A LIFE INTERRUPTED

OSCAR SLADEK

with Corinne Joy Brown

DSEC

Manufactured in the United States of America

Escape To The Tatras
A Boy, A War and A Life Interrupted

Library of Congress Control Number: 2022905499.

ISBN: 978-0-578-38976-9 (pbk)

Interior design by Jorge Enrique Ponce

Cover artwork design by Chris ONeill

Map drawn by Adena Sladek

Cover artwork: Presov 1935 Masarykova Ulica historic postcard (layer) – public domain.
Oscar Sladek portrait (layer): © Oscar Sladek ALL RIGHTS RESERVED.
High Tatras Snow-Capped Mountains photo (layer): licensed via canstockphoto.com

All photos and documents herein are the personal property of the contributing Sladek, Zinger and/or Staub family member(s). All rights are hereby reserved. All other photos, images licenses and/or copyright details are as noted.

Published by
DSEC
8306 Wilshire Boulevard #510 Beverly Hills, California 90211 USA
For information including media, author appearances, interview requests and rights and permissions, please contact: info@escapetothetatras.com

This book is dedicated to my mother, Anyu,
my father, Apu, all of those in our family
who perished in the Holocaust,
and to my loving wife, Selma.

The Denver Post
September 1, 1939

AUTHOR NOTE

Wet, exhausted and cold, I collapsed against the tall man clutching my hand as we paused at the edge of a field. It was a clear night with a full moon. We had walked all day, covering more than a dozen miles by foot through broad fields with no incident, but the last 500 yards of crusty snow across this final open space bordered by a forest would decide our fate.

"You will stay down close to the snow and creep like a rabbit, understand?" he said, his voice barely audible. "If you hear the double hoot of an owl, my signal, it means drop! Lie as flat in the snow as you can. Any wrong move and you could be dead."

The words of my smuggler caused me to shiver, my heart thundering in my chest, and, squinting my eyes, I targeted the dark mass of trees on the far side of the moonlit expanse. I looked straight ahead, hoping to speed through the snow, straight as an arrow. He released my hand, knelt down to show me the exact position, and whispered "Now, go Osika! Go!"

છ

That was the day I left my parents in Slovakia, walked for hours with a man I'd never met before, and crossed secretly into Hungary. That was the day I left my childhood behind, the day everything changed.

It is difficult to imagine the journey of a life when only a young child beginning to explore the world. What happens when that world falls apart and life becomes a struggle to survive is the stuff of books and film. When I was that child, a mere boy caught in the midst of a genocide and the coldest winter ever recorded in Europe, I never imagined I'd be writing this story. In fact, due to the extreme circumstances surrounding my family and myself, I wasn't sure if I would even come out alive.

Now, as a grown man who can look back on a full and remarkable life, I am grateful to have witnessed and triumphed over the unimaginable, so much so that it has confirmed in me a deep and abiding belief —that in spite of all that has happened, in spite of the heartbreak and the loss, I know that every one of us has the capacity to rise up and fulfill our potential —to grow, to love life, and to live with purpose and hope for a better tomorrow.

With gratitude,
Oscar Sladek

Map of Slovakia showing historic and present-day boundaries.
The dashed line indicates the border between Slovakia and Hungary between 1938 and 1945.

1935 postcard of Hlavna Ulica (Main Street), Prešov.
We lived above my parents' store which was located on the right,
and my grandparents lived above their store which was located on the left
adjacent to the front doors of the Cathedral of Saint Nicholas.
Photo: postcard-public domain

By the year 1944 in the city of Prešov, originally located in the eastern half of Czechoslovakia and the place of my birth, life for Jews had come to a terrifying halt. The national government of our renamed "Slovakia", a brand-new country created in 1938 by political division, had recently become a German ally and Jewish life everywhere was in danger. Eastern Slovakia was home to an estimated 300,000 people at the time with a sizeable Jewish population. Prešov once had a community of some 4500 Jewish souls. By including the surrounding towns, the number was closer to 6000.

The Nazi invasion into Slovakia in August of '44 triggered a national uprising. As a result, fierce paramilitary guards of the new Slovakian Fascist regime patrolled our streets day and night, bent on suppressing insurrection. Earlier, in September of 1940, a German officer named Dieter Wisliceny, an advisor to the Slovak government, was appointed to deal with the "Jewish Question", the forced removal of the Jewish citizens of Slovakia. He was instructed by Berlin to lay out his plans to dislocate all 90,000 Slovakian Jews, as well as strip them of their belongings, wealth and civil rights.

The city of Prešov was the testing ground and in 1941, became the first Slovakian city to impose anti-Jewish laws. These were presented in what was called "The Jewish Codex", a set of rules and regulations prohibiting public gatherings, attendance or instruction at schools or universities, and the holding of personal bank accounts, employment, or ownership of property—restrictions of every kind spelled out in 270 grueling paragraphs. It was also here where the word *"Žid"* or Jew was first defined as a race, changing the definition of a dignified people who had long upheld an ancient religion.

At that time, my family and all of Prešov's remaining Jewish residents, had been forced to wear yellow armbands, and soon after, yellow stars on all their clothes. One by one, they had been robbed of nearly all their personal freedoms. By 1941, all Jewish businesses had been taken over by non-Jews, and as a final blow, many of us witnessed the destruction by fire of our beloved Beth Abraham synagogue.

According to historical records, by the war's end, the Fascist government had succeeded in rounding up and deporting approximately 80,000 Slovakian Jews to labor or extermination camps. The seeds of this disastrous catastrophe had been sewn when the Versailles Treaty, signed in 1919 and marking the end of World War I, changed the geographic landscape of Europe. Heavy bargaining among the nations who were the winners and losers of that war created new alliances and federations. One of those newly established republics was Czechoslovakia, created overnight in 1922 from four former ethnically-similar but separate nations: the Czechs (also known as Bohemians), the Moravians, the Ruthenians (located between Slovakia and the Ukraine) and the Slovaks. As they were neighbors and part of the Slavic group of nations with similar languages, it justified their unification.

From the beginning, Czechoslovakia established itself as a model Western democracy. Minorities, including Jews, were given full rights of citizenship. The new country was ruled by a representative government based in Prague. Regional governments in the cities of Brno and Bratislava were also established with limited powers. In 1922, Tomaš G. Masaryk, our first president, was elected. But our fledgling democracy, so full of hope, was to be short-lived. Czechoslovakia was to become a pawn in Adolf Hitler's rise to power.

The dire circumstances of the following story are only partial events in what was to become the worst tragedy to befall all of Europe— perhaps, the entire world. In the year 1944, having held on longer than most in our vanishing community, none of the adults in my immediate family could believe that their worst fears had been realized. Wherever they looked, German-controlled Slovak militia surrounded us, determined to oust any remaining Jewish citizens from every single home, business, school or synagogue. Slovakian Jews were doomed. It seemed there was no way out. The miraculous survival of my father Bedrich, my mother Irene, and myself, Oskar Štaub, would take courage, creativity and luck.

Sarlota Irene Grünfeld (left, my mother), with her sister Rözsi (right), and her husband Armyn (center). His mother is seated. c. 1932

My paternal great-grandmother Maria Degner Czigler (left) and her little sister, Linka, c. 1870

CHAPTER 1

In The Beginning

Μy ancestors first settled in the region of eastern Slovakia some-time around the start of the seventeenth century. At that time, it was a territory of the Austro-Hungarian monarchy, which permitted mi-norities of the Jewish faith to settle there. With the passage of time, their contributions to the local economy earned them increased freedom, privileges and greater acceptance in the dominant Chris-tian society.

A large family of Jews settled in the town of Sobrance. My mater-nal grand-parents, Joseph and Hermina Grünfeld, were hardwork-ing, pious people, dedicated to the tenets of Orthodox Judaism. Per tradition, they believed in raising many children. Their family of offspring totaled thirteen, including my mother Sarlota, who later changed her name to Irene.

About one hour to the northwest by train lived the Štaub family in the town of Prešov. Prešov's Jews had long made many contribu-tions to the physical and cultural assets of the city. Among them was "Neptune's Fountain", a beautiful attraction adorned by many sculptures in the town center that was donated in the 1800s by the city's first Jewish citizen, businessman Marek Hollánder.

My paternal grandparents, Jakub and Henrietta Štaub, known as my "Opapa and Omama", proudly maintained their Jewish traditions, but to a lesser degree. They considered themselves Neolog or Reform in their religious practices. Raising a large family was a religious requirement to be fulfilled, so they had four children, among them my father Bedrich, nicknamed Frici. German was their language of preference over Slovak or Hungarian. As their children were growing up, Jakub and Henrietta encouraged them to be more universal and open-minded than Orthodox Jews in their daily lives, values and beliefs. All the Štaub children, (Arnost, Teodor, Bedrich and Ružena) pursued higher education, loved to travel, befriended non-Jews and followed religious laws selectively.

The Grünfelds, by contrast, were more insulated. Like most who observed Orthodox Jewish traditions, the men prayed daily, kept strict dietary laws, traveled in Jewish circles, and followed the holy commandments to the last letter. Their heads were always covered as a sign of respect to the Almighty. The girls were raised to be good wives, housekeepers and mothers to many future offspring. At home, they spoke primarily Hungarian. They also spoke Yiddish, a form of German and Hebrew, a language common to Jews of Eastern Europe. Joseph studied the Torah and the Talmud daily. Hermina had her hands full raising the children, cooking and maintaining the household. The boys worked with their father in their seltzer factory. Sadly, my grandfather Joseph, who I never knew, died at the age of 57 from heart failure.

Born in 1914 at the beginning of World War I, Irene was the youngest of the Grünfeld daughters. In the summer of 1932 at the age of eighteen she visited the Slovak city of Košice to see relatives. There she was introduced to Frici, the eldest son of the Štaub family. According to family legend, Frici became mesmerized by Irene's beauty, especially her dazzling smile and sparkling brown eyes. She, however, already had a suitor in her town and didn't show any interest.

Frici was a thirty-year-old, attractive bachelor and an accomplished musician. He still lived with his parents, not uncommon in those days. During the week, he helped manage their retail store, located just steps away from the Cathedral of Saint Nicholas, the most central point in Presov, a consummate location. Frici assisted in selling stringed instruments, quality leather goods, records and record players. On the weekends he played his violin with a trio in Prešov's most popular coffee house, the Berger. He also played first violin in the symphony orchestra and conducted the region's military band. He was also a well-known, talented, and respected composer and conductor.

After he met Irene, Frici couldn't get her out of his mind. He was determined to attract her attention. So, every couple of weeks, with his violin under his arm, he would ride the train from Prešov to Sobrance. There, under the window of her bedroom, he would stand outside and play the most romantically beautiful gypsy melodies and other classical pieces until she would be tempted to invite him into her home. Slowly and skillfully, he won her heart.

The two sets of parents met to discuss the details of the Orthodox wedding scheduled for February 19, 1933. The dowry was agreed upon and, when all religious matters were clarified and any stumbling blocks removed, a lively wedding celebration was held on the scheduled date in the city of Košice, attended by many family members and friends. The ceremony took place at the home of Ella and Moric Zinger. Ella was Irene's older sister who was already married.

A great deal of gossip followed the much-publicized wedding. People referred to it from the start as an unlikely union of two young Jews, miles apart in the practice of their religion. Some skeptics viewed it as a mixed marriage that would never last. But Frici and Irene were very much in love. Several weeks later Irene became pregnant. They leased a modern apartment in Prešov and Irene furnished it with imported furniture from Italy. She possessed an innate talent for creating an attractive home, and dressing fashionably. She was driven to succeed using her beauty, people skills and common sense.

Next, Frici opened a business with funds from Irene's dowry, a store similar to the one his parents had operated for the previous twenty-some years, and on the same street. The merchandise consisted of fine imported leather goods, toys, musical instruments, record players and records. Most items were made in Germany, a source of quality products. The store was located on the main street called *Masarykova Ulica*, across the street from St. John the Baptist Greek Orthodox Church.

Irene's charming personality, alongside that of Frici, the well-known musician, attracted customers from the entire eastern Šariš region of Slovakia. Irene was skilled in selling the leather handbags, wallets, briefcases and suitcases, while Frici took pleasure in selling the many violins, guitars, percussion instruments and records. He was especially fond of his gypsy (Romani) customers who were musicians by nature. Over time, the Štaub family cornered the city of Prešov's retail market in leather goods and musical instruments. Together, they began to build a business that would guide them into a bright and promising future.

Meanwhile, also in 1933, ill winds had begun to blow across all of Europe. Few realized the underlying damage done by World War I. Germany had lost the war, was left with a shattered economy and searched for whom to blame. This was made only worse by the worldwide economic depression of the 1930s. The Jews of Germany and elsewhere were branded by the extreme right-wing as wealth mongers and Communists. As Germany reorganized and seized power, the new Chancellor Adolf Hitler was determined to cleanse Germany and all of Europe of Bolsheviks, Jews, gypsies, persons with physical or intellectual disabilities, homosexuals and other "undesirables", and create a pure Aryan society for the new empire of the Third Reich.

It was then, in this daunting environment, that I, Oskar Štaub, was to come into the world, just two years into Hitler's diabolical rise to power.

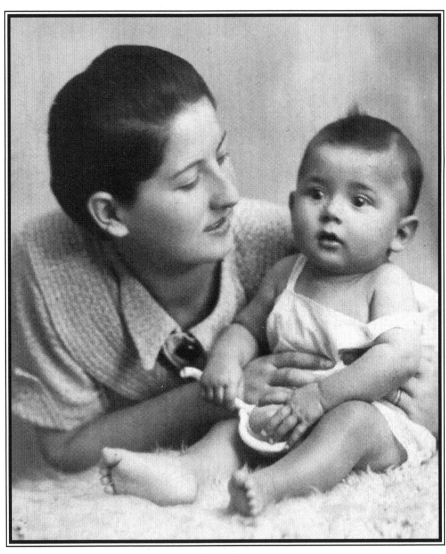

My mother and me, 1935

My parents, Bedrich 'Frici' and Sarlota 'Irene'
in Prešov, 1945

The Štaub Family
Presov, c. 1935
Top row L-R: My father, Bedrich with his sister Ružena and brother Arnošt.
Bottom row L-R: my grandmother Henrietta, youngest child Teodor, and my grandfather Jakub.

CHAPTER 2

Oskar

Close to midnight on March 18, 1935, my mother, Irene Štaub, gave birth to her first and only child — me, a healthy boy with deep brown eyes and coal black hair. My parents named me Oskar. Eight days later I was circumcised according to Jewish tradition, surrounded by immediate family and friends. I was also named Chaim Yosef in memory of my mother's deceased father. And this is how I came into being.

I was born into a Jewish family and thus was entered and recorded in the Prešov city archives as Oskar Štaub-ISR. ISR was an abbreviation for Israelite, a term that in Europe referred to a Jewish person. Unbeknownst to me, those three letters, "ISR", in my birth certificate became, within a few short years, a mark of condemnation bestowed on me by circumstances I could not avoid.

An early memory takes me back to my years as a toddler. I was approximately two years old and standing in my crib, holding on to the side rail staring at a double door made of opaque glass. It was not very transparent but I remember seeing silhouettes of my parents and their friends on the other side, sitting around a table in the adjoining family room, playing card games and smoking cigarettes. The smoke irritated my eyes as it seeped under the door. I jumped up and down, wanting my mother, Anyu. I kept calling for her over and over until, feeling frustrated, I began to cry. The sound of my distress grew louder.

As I cried, I jumped up and down on the mattress, trying to bang on the glass door but my hands could not reach it. My anger intensified as my cries increased. The tantrum endured for a long while. Suddenly, the door opened, Anyu entered, spanked me on my bottom, and told me to lie down and go to sleep.

"It's late," she said. "Shhhhh. Don't disturb us!" She left, closing the door behind her. I tried to sleep but could not. The loud talking, laughing and the smacking of cards on the table kept me up. I cried some more until I became exhausted and fell asleep.

The next morning, I remember awakening to the muffled sounds of my parents moving about. Anyu dressed me, getting me ready for the day. She gave me kisses and hugs. My father, whom I called Apu in Hungarian, left our courtyard apartment for our store. Anyu always took longer to dress and fix her hair and make-up. Soon, my German-born nanny arrived. She received her daily instructions from my mother who also reminded me to be a good boy and do as I was told. Then she left for work. As you might deduct by now, I grew up speaking many different languages, thanks to my grandparents, parents and caregivers.

Nanny fed me breakfast, then took me for a walk in the long interior courtyard. I liked kicking my rubber ball and running after it, also chasing after roaming cats, especially pulling their tails. Sometimes, they snarled back at me and scratched my hand, making me cry.

Eating lunch was often an unpleasant experience. Cooked spinach was served every day, prescribed by the pediatrician. I couldn't stand it. So instead of swallowing, I held it in my mouth. Nanny got angry. She threatened, "I will tell your muti [*mother*] that you were a bad boy today. You would not eat your spinach!" I wanted to cry but couldn't with a mouthful of spinach. Eventually, I spit it out on the tray of my highchair and began to wail. She usually grabbed me and spanked me. It hurt, and I cried even louder.

On the days when I was a good boy, Nanny took me for a walk on the tree-lined street alongside our apartment building. There I saw people walking, some with dogs, and they let me touch them. I was always scared of the big ones. "Some dogs bite," she told me. "*Achtung!*," she said in German. (Be careful.) Not surprisingly, the first language I learned was German, Nanny's mother tongue.

Shortly after my second birthday, I was diagnosed with a hearing loss due to a painful ear infection. Doctors felt certain I had a fifty percent chance of losing all my hearing, and back then, we had no antibiotics or penicillin. Instead, they performed a delicate surgery called a mastoidectomy that left a hole in my skull behind both ears. Luckily, I recovered fully and regained my hearing.

One of the most exciting things for me was to see a horse-drawn carriage, especially when we walked on the main street. In winter when the road was covered with snow, the horses pulled large sleds with people sitting inside. On special occasions, Anyu and Apu would visit friends and we all got into a sled. I loved hearing the bells ring around the horses' necks as they strained to pull.

At the opposite end of our courtyard was a beauty shop. Sometimes Anyu took me in with her. It was a very exciting place for a toddler. Inside, near the door, were coat racks and low on the wall, springy clips for client's umbrellas. I liked to click the clips. It made a sound like "putt, putt." After a while, the ladies got annoyed and Anyu would tell me to stop but within a few minutes, I would get bored doing nothing, so I returned to the same mischief. I would yell "putt-put" and the ladies screamed at me to stop!

Sometimes my grandmother, Omama Hermina (Anyu's mother), came to stay with us. She hugged me a lot and gave me sloppy kisses and often, just annoyed me. I liked to jump up and down our front steps. The most fun was to jump from the top landing over the steps and down to the bottom pavement. When she saw me doing this she would scream, "Ooy, ooy, this boy is going to kill himself." And I kept jumping. I liked to scare her. The more she yelled, the more I jumped.

I always had nice toys to play with because Anyu and Apu also sold toys in their store. Every year they gave me new ones for my birthday. Anyu also bought me nice shirts, pants and sweaters. She loved nice clothes. My father wore a suit in the store, always very business-like, but on the weekends, was more casual. At home, he liked to play his violin to relax.

Once in a while, my parents took me to a large hall to hear a big band play music. Sometimes I liked it and sometimes I got bored. But I liked it best when my Apu played with his band. My favorite instrument back then was the drum. I could feel the rhythm in my body. If I heard a new rhythm, I could repeat it with my fingers on a wooden chair or door. Many times, I opened a door and tapped out all kinds of rhythms with my fingers on both hands, left hand outside, right hand inside. Sometimes I pretended to play the trumpet too. I invented all kinds of melodies. Slow or fast, I was often very loud and my parents made me stop.

Most of all, I liked to listen to Apu playing his violin. He used to tell me that he must practice and learn new songs all the time. He played so beautifully. I could have listened to him all day. He played and stopped, played and stopped, and wrote musical notes all the while on a sheet of paper with lots of lines. When I inquired what he was doing he would say, "I am writing a new song, Osika." I wished I could write songs like him, never dreaming that one day when I grew up, I actually would.

1936

My father Apu playing the violin. He was a gifted and popular composer, conductor and
musician. Several of his songs were commercially recorded by well-known
singers on ESTA records. He also frequently performed at Prešov's Café Berger.

Phonograph label: SUPRAPHON a.s., 1938

CHAPTER 3

Growing Up in Prešov

As I grew older, Anyu often dressed me up on Sundays in nice woolen clothes which I hated. I was allergic to wool and still am, but that is what children wore in those days. I didn't have a choice. I would try to forget my suffering when she took me to the main street to a long, narrow park with lots of room to run. I liked picking the tiny yellow flowers that grew there in the summer in the high, green grass. Often, I took a net with me and tried to catch a butterfly. I liked chasing them, but those butterflies were faster than I was. When I did succeed, I liked to play with it and then release it. Sometimes, when I was in a naughty mood and no one was watching, I tore off the butterfly's wings and watched it walk around in circles. Then I felt bad, but I never told anybody what I did.

My favorite days were Saturday and Sunday when we got together with family and friends. Our lives revolved around Jewish customs and holidays and we observed the Jewish Sabbath every week from Friday sundown to Saturday sundown.

On Friday night, at the beginning of our Shabbat and before it grew dark, Anyu would cover her head, light two candles and say a prayer in Hebrew, gently waving her hands in a circle over the flames. This was a way of welcoming in our day of rest, observed all day Saturday. Lighting candles was followed by a special dinner. I liked watching her. I never said a word as I watched her perform this mysterious traditional Shabbat ritual that I learned to love. To me, she was bringing the candles to life. Afterwards, she would give me a hug and a kiss and say, "Good Shabbes my Osika," using a Yiddish version of the word Shabbat.

Next, we all sat around the Shabbat table and per our tradition, Apu lifted a shiny goblet and read a prayer from a special prayer book called a *siddur*. He sang a beautiful melody to the words written in Hebrew. When he was done, he took a sip of wine and then passed the goblet to Anyu. I was the last one to take a tiny sip. The wine tasted sweet and I liked it. Dinner followed, but first Apu recited a *hamotzi*, a prayer over the challa, a special sweet, braided bread we ate only on Shabbat. It tasted yummy. Before we started to eat the gefilte fish, a chopped fish delicacy made with onions and matzo meal, Apu washed his hands and again, said another short prayer in Hebrew that ended with the words *netilas yodoim* (blessing for washing of the hands.) Then came the soup. Round circles of chicken grease floated on top. Too much fat. I couldn't eat much of it.

Anyu was very proud of her cooking. She kept telling me to eat more but I resisted which annoyed her. We had an ongoing battle over my eating habits. My taste buds were very selective and I didn't like many foods. I couldn't stand cooked onion for example, and I hated potato soup. When beef was tough, chewing was difficult. But spinach was always my number one food enemy. It made me gag. I liked chicken best, especially the *pulke* (leg), the *gorgle* (neck), the liver and the chicken feet. I could hardly wait to eat small chicken eggs, a delicacy. Lentil soup was my absolute favorite. So was *cholent*, a flavorful beef, potato and bean, slow-cooked stew. Every Friday, Anyu took me with her to the kosher bakery to pick up her large pot of cholent that had been cooking in the bakery's big oven overnight.

On Thursdays, she sometimes took me to the fish store to retrieve a live trout from a large tub with all sizes of fish swimming in it. Catching them in the water was a challenge. I always tried to catch one but it would slide out of my hands. Finally, Anyu grabbed one and bought it and then we hurried home to let it swim in our bathtub. The scary part was when Apu came home, took it outside, and hit the fish's head with a metal tool until it died. I didn't like that. It always upset me.

After the meal, Anyu and Apu sang songs and prayers in Hebrew. I tried to sing along but didn't know all the words. On Friday nights we went to sleep early because we had to rise early in the morning to go to the synagogue. Anyu dressed me on those occasions since my Nanny didn't come on Shabbat. We all wore nice clothes and walked there together. Anyu always held my hand. Apu carried his *tallis* (prayer shawl) in a special bag.

In the synagogue the men sat downstairs and the women upstairs in the balcony. I'd rather not have been with the men because if I sat next to Apu, I could not leave. I had to sit quietly and behave. Once in a while I could stand up when everybody else stood up. When I got antsy and restless, Apu gave in and let me go. He always told me to go upstairs to Anyu. I liked walking up and down the wooden stairs. The ladies smiled at me. Anyu liked to have me near her. She always straightened out my clothes and then combed my hair backwards so I would look neat and presentable. She also wanted my hairline to grow higher off my forehead. As much as I hated it, I wore a hair net to bed every night to make it grow the way she wanted.

When I got bored at services, I told her I wanted to go back to sit with Apu. But actually, I would slip out the back door to the courtyard. Usually, some of my friends would be playing *pitkes* (marbles) with small, colored glass balls. We would sit on the floor in a circle and take our turns. The older boys played soccer in the courtyard, but I was still too small to play with them. *When I grow up,* I always thought, *I'll be on a team like them.*

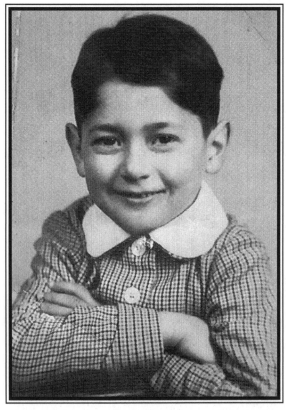

Oskar Štaub
1938

CHAPTER 4

A War Is Coming

Aftter lunch on Saturday afternoons, we usually visited Anyu and
Apu's friends. I was always happy when we visited Olga *néni* (Aunt
Olga), Anyu's very best friend, because I liked to play with her daughter Eva. We were the same age. We were supposed to start going to
school together the next year. Our favorite game was hide-and-seek,
or we played dominoes.

In our courtyard I liked to play with my *karika*, a thin wooden
wheel which I moved with a stick along the paved path. At home I
liked to play with miniature metal soldiers or cowboys and Indians
that we sold in our store. We also sold model tanks, trucks and cannons. Apu told me they were all made in Germany. It was fun to set
up two armies to fight against each other.

Once, on the shortwave radio we owned, I heard about the German army marching into Prague, the capital of Czechoslovakia. So, I
gave my armies names. One was the Czechoslovak army and the other the German army. I often heard my parents speak to their friends
about a man named Hitler. They said that he was very dangerous and
that he hated the Jewish people. They heard he wanted to start a big

23

war. Many times they whispered to each other because they didn't want me to hear what they were saying. When I got close to where they were talking to each other, someone always said *der yingele* (*the child*) in Yiddish, and then they stopped talking altogether.

One day we all heard a long, loud, foreign sound blast over the city. Everyone went outside to listen. It sounded like a trumpet but much louder. When it finally stopped, Anyu told me that it was a siren and would be sounded each time before airplanes flew over Prešov as a warning. "When that happens," she said, "we will have to go down to the *pince* (cellar)."

I remembered seeing a plane flying over Prešov the year before. It had no roof, like a big bird with metal wings. It was the first time I saw a flying machine. I could see a man sitting in the plane and waving, so I waved back to him. The plane made a loud noise and flew low over the city. I was afraid that it might fall down on me. The pilot kept flying in a circle and then disappeared and never came back. It all seemed like magic.

In our store I liked to play with a small toy airplane. I would wind it up and watch it roll around and around on the wooden floor in a circle. Another toy airplane that also wound up did somersaults, flipping this way and that, but the one that circled was more fun. How I wished they could fly like the real one I saw up in the air. That would have been something!

Once I got into a lot of trouble. I was playing in our courtyard and saw a rock lying on the ground. I liked to pick up rocks and see how far I could throw them. I looked around, saw no one, and quickly picked it up, wondering if I could throw it over the brick wall that separated our courtyard from the one next door. I hurled it up, heard it hit the wall and then fall to the ground. I did it again. No luck. By the fourth time it went over the wall —boom! I heard a glass shattering. I broke a window. I panicked! I ran quickly to our apartment and started playing with my toys. Then I heard a man's voice cursing. It was that nasty caretaker from next door. He came looking for me saying, "I want to lay my hands on the little devil and beat the daylights out of him!"

Nanny was ironing at that moment. I ran and quickly slid under my parents' bed. She came looking for me and when she heard the neighbor yelling in the courtyard, she went out and told him, "It couldn't have been Osi. He's been in the apartment all this time playing with his toys."

The man calmed down and left. But the next day he got hold of my parents and carried on like a crazy person. In the end, I confessed to Anyu that I had hurled a rock over the wall but did not know there was a building nearby. My parents ended up paying for the repair of the window. Luckily, the man did not catch and punish me; that was the last time I threw a rock into the unknown.

When I turned six, I started going to public school. By this time, our country had a new name. It changed from Czechoslovakia to

Slovenská Republika (Slovak Republic). With the elections of 1938, we had become a friend, or ally, of nearby Germany, a big country run by Adolf Hitler's National Socialist Worker's Party elected in 1933. Before that we had a kind and decent government, a democracy. Now, according to my father, we were a Fascist government with many new rules that made life more difficult.

For the first few days of school, Anyu walked with me and after that, I would pick up my friend Eva and we walked together. School was fun. In my class were boys and girls and my best friends were Jewish. My favorite class was music. I took part in the choir because I already loved to sing. I also liked physical education. I especially liked to run and jump over hurdles.

Before Christmas, I rehearsed with the choir. Some parts of songs I would sing solo because the teacher liked my voice. Even so, Anyu was unhappy about me singing Christmas music. She told me I was not allowed to say the names of Jesus and Mary. After the program, many parents came to me and complimented me on my vocal skills. I felt so good and proud. I liked that special feeling.

My friend and 'schoolmate' Eva Nagy survived the Holocaust in a convent.
Her parents were captured and killed by the Nazi soldiers. c. 1941

Adolf Hitler & Jozef Tiso
Jozef Tiso, Slovak politician and Roman Catholic Priest who served as President of the
Slovak Republic, a client state of Nazi Germany during WWII from 1939-1945. In 1947,
after the war, he was executed for war crimes and crimes against humanity in Bratislava.
Photo: public domain

CHAPTER 5

The Fascist Regime and New Laws 1942

Many things changed once I reached the second grade. I was required to wear a yellow star on my clothes along with all the other Jewish children in my school. When I was born, our President was Tomaš Masaryk, a democratic leader, and school children sang the Czecho-Slovak anthem. The new president of Slovakia was named Jozef Tiso, an authoritarian Catholic priest, and we sang a new song in school *"Nad Tatrou sa Blýzka Hromy Divo Biju"* ("Over the Tatra Mountains, the Lightning and Thunder Beat Wildly"). I liked the old one better. *"Kde Domov Můj"* (*"Where My Home Is"*).

I didn't like my second-grade teacher at all. He was very strict and many times sent me to stand in the corner for a long time. I didn't make trouble but sometimes he would lean over and twist my ear until I begged him to stop. He used to hit me with his ruler on my fingertips too. I thought he didn't like me because I wore the yellow Star of David. I didn't like school anymore. My classmates made fun of me and called me bad names with the word Jew in them. They told me to go away to Palestine or else Hitler was going to come and get me. After school, they taunted me and, some days, two or three kids actually beat me up. I tried to fight back but they always tripped me and I ended up on the ground. If I was lucky, some parent would stop them from harassing me. If not, I often arrived home crying with my clothes soiled or even torn.

Anyu and Apu tried to console me. Most of the time I was sad and angry with my schoolmates and teachers and didn't understand why Apu couldn't straighten it all out so things were like they were before.

By the time I turned seven years of age, life in my city had changed a lot. Nanny had stopped coming and I seldom went to school. The store on *Hlavna Ulica* became my home-away-from-home and Anyu took me with her when she went to work.

Anyu told me never to cross this big street alone under any circumstances and to stay away from the Slavic Orthodox church. Hlavna Ulica was the biggest and longest street in all of Prešov and offered a lot to see. A few doors away from the store, in the entry way of a courtyard, a horse was hitched to a large, round stone which ground up wheat stalks. I liked to stand in front of the double-gate and watch the horse walk round and round. After a while, I felt sorry for the poor animal.

The street was always busy. Many people walked on the side-walks and many *fiakers* (carriages)and other types of horse-drawn wagons drove by. Most of them were pulled by one horse. The fancy fiakers had two horses. Every so often, a religious procession passed on foot or a funeral came by with a horse-drawn hearse leading the procession.

Once in a while, a car or a truck rolled along making a lot of noise and smoke. Most of the trucks belonged to the Slovak military. Only rich people drove cars. Sometimes a spooked, loose horse galloped free on the main street with men chasing after, trying to catch it. When this happened, it scared everyone. Most of the people on the sidewalk hid in courtyards or quickly entered the stores for safety. Once, I was crossing the street when, out of nowhere, a two-horse carriage came upon me. I couldn't get out of the way fast enough and was swept up between the two giant horses' connected harness. Luckily, I grabbed onto the harness' wooden yoke between them and saved myself from being trampled to death underfoot. My mother was screaming loudly for the driver to stop because he had no idea I was there. He couldn't see me. I never crossed the street by myself again.

The railway station was not very far, so when a train arrived in Prešov many people walked or rode by our store on their way to the center of the city. In the winter, I loved to see them in large, horse-drawn sleds, covered with blankets. The traffic was very quiet then, and after it grew dark, almost every corner had a handcart with a small oven baking chestnuts called *gáštane* in Slovak. Apu and Anyu loved to eat them, fresh from the coal-fired oven, warm and delicious. I liked them too. Before Christmas it was always great fun to walk along the main street at night. All kinds of costumed characters could be seen, singing, carrying bells and big crosses. Sometimes I got a little frightened by them, especially the ones who had too much to drink and staggered around the sidewalks. Best of all, colorful holiday lights and pretty decorations lit up the streets everywhere.

Anxiously we greeted the spring of 1942. My parents were very worried. By that time, people gathered silently, not speaking to each other. We spent much more time at home. Anyu said I dared not be seen by any of the bad people who wanted to hurt Jews. Members of the newly formed Slovakian national guard carrying rifles patrolled our town, hauling Jewish people out of their homes at random and down to the train station. They were called the *Hlinkova Garda* (Hlinka Guardists), a kind of tough police force organized by the Fascist government. Awful things were happening everywhere. One day, Apu was walking on the street. By mistake, he wore one of his coats missing the required yellow Star of David. One of his customers recognized him, yelled at him, and punched him right in the face. Poor Apu came home all shaken and bruised.

I overheard Anyu and Apu talking to their Jewish friends about the disruptive things occurring everywhere. "It's never been this bad," said Apu. "No one is safe here anymore."

"We should have left when we could," answered his friend, another musician. "Wherever we go, we are hunted now."

They told me that Apu's parents, Omama and Opapa Štaub, had

to move out of their apartment because of a new law that said Jews were no longer allowed to live on our street, now renamed *Hlinkova Ulica*. (It was hard to keep up. Everything kept changing.) Their long-time maid and housekeeper took their nice home instead, switching places. She moved permanently into their beautiful, second-floor apartment and they moved into her much smaller dwelling, a kind of cottage apartment in a smaller building at the other end of the courtyard.

This new anti-Jewish law was one of many. For example, now any non-Jew could go to the City Hall and buy a permit to take over a Jewish business. Then, another law was posted stating that no Jews could even own a business. All of this was a terrible blow to the Jews of Prešov, a community dating back to the 1780s. Now, no Jewish professional such as a doctor or lawyer could practice, no teacher could teach, no musicians could perform, and all Jewish bank accounts were seized, a polite way to say "legally stolen." Fortunately, many Jewish households kept money and valuables hidden away for instances just like this.

My parent's very close Christian friend, Dr. Jozef Šolc, an attorney who was the Prešov District Judge and therefore quite influential in the community, recommended that his younger sister Maria purchase a permit from city hall to take over our family store. She did and we received a document stating that "at a specific date, she would be in charge, but could keep my parents on as employees." This privilege was extended via a special permit because they had "necessary knowledge." She took possession of the store and privately promised to give it back to us when everything returned to normal.

By this time, all the new laws had stripped us of our basic freedoms. The bank had seized our savings and I overheard my parents discussing how concerned they were about our future. Anyu believed that we too would soon have to vacate our apartment that used to be located across the street from my grandparents. I wondered where we were going to move.

It didn't take us long to find out.

My beloved paternal grandparents of blessed memory
Henrietta (Czigler) and Jakub Štaub, c. 1900

Members of our family worshipped at the Prešov Orthodox Synagogue
which was vandalized during the fascist era. It has been beautifully restored
with financial contributions from survivors living abroad and today it houses
the Permanent Judaic Exposition and is known as the Museum of Jewish Culture.

Forced out of our homes and businesses, we lived secretly in my grandparents
housekeeper's quarters, tucked behind their storefront.

CHAPTER 6

Life with Omama and Opapa Štaub

Since my parents and I were unable to find a suitable apartment off the main street (as required by the new law), we were invited to move in with Omama and Opapa in the maid's quarters. They used one room and we lived in the other. Sadly, they also lost their business and apartment, both of which were taken over by strangers.

Anyu and Omama shared the small kitchen which had an old stove and oven. Many times, I went to the shed in the center of the big courtyard to fill a bucket with coal and bring it back to the kitchen. In some ways, it was more fun for me to live there and help out with all kinds of chores which I never did in our former home.

In the spring, I watched Omama feed a large white goose with corn. She sat on a low stool outside with the goose's neck between her knees. With one hand she held the beak open, with the other she kept pushing the corn kernels into its throat, force feeding it, so it should get nice and fat before Pesach (the holiday of Passover). I couldn't stand it! She was forcing the kernels down its throat. I told her not to hurt the poor bird, but she was relentless. The goose kept choking and finally I had to leave.

The poor, overfed goose was ritually slaughtered and prepared for the Passover festive meals – the Seders. The dead, naked bird, stuffed with tasty matza stuffing, was placed on a giant platter in the middle of the table. Anyu put a plate of food in front of me and urged me to eat the delicious baked goose meat she and Omama cooked together. I could not eat, unable to get the sight of the choking goose out of my mind. That was not the only thing that bothered me. I hated the Seders. The endless readings in Hebrew bored me to tears. I was not allowed to leave the table. Everyone drank wine except me. I was the only child around a bunch of anxious, somber adults.

At this Seder our prayers and songs had to be sung very softly. We spoke in hushed and guarded tones. Further, all the windows were covered with dark fabric to prevent any leakage of light to the yard. Every so often someone uttered the warning words "*chit-chuck*" meaning "let's be quiet" in Hungarian. Nerves became stretched like rubber bands as we all heard the sound of boots scraping the narrow path in the courtyard —perhaps the dreaded Hlinka Guardists on their way to the back gate. Thankfully, the footsteps grew fainter. For a couple of minutes no one around the table breathed. Then we all exhaled and the readings continued. Another blessing was said over the cup of wine. By the end of the Seder, the adults had drunk four cups of wine, eaten a four-course dinner and had a lesson in Jewish history starting with slavery in Egypt and the Exodus, and ending with speculative theories about the outcome of the current world war. But by the time I went to bed, I was totally rattled by the scare we experienced and unable to fall asleep for the longest while.

My Omama Hermina, Anyu's mother, stopped coming to stay with us. She went to live with Aunt Ella, her other daughter, and her husband, Uncle Moric, who lived in Kassa, a city not far away. Kassa used to be a Slovak city called Košice but now, due to our newly assigned borders, it became part of Hungary. Anyu told me that life in Kassa was better and Jewish people didn't have to wear yellow stars on their clothes. Omama would be much happier there. I wondered if we would be, too.

I celebrated my seventh birthday on March 18, 1942. Anyu baked my favorite cookies called *pogátče* which were rich and buttery like shortbread. The family sang "Happy Birthday", I got many kisses and hugs and a few toys, plus a couple boxes of colored pencils. I enjoyed drawing pictures, mostly houses, trees, mountains and clouds. I wanted to learn how to draw animal faces which was not so easy. Once I stopped going to school, Apu helped me with addition, subtraction, and spelling. We worked on spelling mostly by reading stories. Then, he would ask me questions about them. I also had to memorize poems and blessings in Hebrew.

I was sad that I could not have a pet. Once I had a cute little dog called Muki. One day we played hide-and-seek outside in the courtyard. Without any warning, he took off and ran out the gate to the main street. I started running after him but Anyu yelled at me not to. "Osika, stop! It's dangerous for you to be out there." I listened to her and stopped, but my Muki never came back. It made me lonesome and sad for a long time. I loved my Muki. He was a good friend. Why did he run away?

As a Christian, my grandparents' housekeeper, Maria, risked her own personal safety to help my family survive for which I am eternally grateful.

CHAPTER 7

Hiding

Once the war started, the adults listened attentively to the weekly BBC news (British Broadcast Corporation) on our secret radio. It was forbidden to own one so we kept it hidden. I was made to understand that it was strictly against the law to own one and if the *Gardisti*, the local police, ever found out about it they would take us all to jail. We turned out the lights and sat close by the speaker, turned down to a very low volume. Uncle Teodor, who we called Tidi, Apu's youngest brother who was staying with us, was the only one who understood English, so he translated.

The worst time for me was when they listened to Radio Berlin and the weekly broadcast of speeches in German by the man they called the Führer, Adolf Hitler. He was always shouting, and even on low volume, his voice boomed like thunder. It scared me. I could understand some of the words in German and they were hateful and mean. He was always angry at something, especially the Bolsheviks, and always the Jews. Over and over, I heard him say he wanted to rid Germany of all foreigners and anyone he thought were enemies of the German people. I always felt like he was talking directly to me, even coming after me. Following his speeches, I would have a hard time falling asleep. Sometimes, I had terrible nightmares and was afraid Hitler would send his soldiers to snatch me and lock me up in a dark jail cell.

The adults around me got very upset when the broadcast was over, and I could hear the men argue. "Bah, he is just barking!" said my Opapa. "He can't hurt us. But thanks to him, we are all learning how to live in fear."

"He is determined to destroy us," said Omama. "I have heard his armies are taking over entire cities. Jews by the thousands are being deported. It is a disaster."

My mother used to shake her head in disbelief. She looked worried. Sometimes tears welled up in her eyes. I often tried to comfort her by laying my head on her shoulder. "Don't worry, Anyu," I used to say and would take her hand.

Mostly, we kept the windows shuttered and whispered to each other when we spoke, reacting swiftly to any sounds that might mean danger to our safety. My heart beat hard and fast when we heard a knock at our door. Anyu would put her finger to her lips to indicate that no one should make a sound and we would not answer, pretending no one was at home. I usually held my breath until whoever was there went away. Many false alarms created unbearably tense moments. More than once, Anyu whispered to me, "Quick! Go hide under the bed!" and I always did.

We were fortunate that the Šolc family helped us escape the persecutions. They were more than kind, as well as respectful and compassionate. One day we received an advance warning from Judge Šolc of an imminent, random round-ups of Jews in Prešov. He always warned us by delivering a message in a sealed envelope via his secretary. Terrified, we knew then we had to find someplace to hide. That evening, after dark, we walked cautiously to the home of my parents' Christian friends, good people who had befriended us years earlier. Before we knocked on the door, we had to make sure that none of the other neighbors saw us there. When all was clear, and they welcomed us in, we quickly slipped into the entrance.

In the corner of the kitchen, they lifted up a carpet that revealed a wooden trap door. Then they hurried us down a few steps into an unfinished dugout under the house, just a hollow of earth and rock. They passed down some blankets, and somehow, curled together, we stayed there overnight. Breathing was difficult for lack of oxygen. It was so dark and cold it was like being buried alive! I was so scared I couldn't sleep. I hugged Anyu most of the night.

The next day they lowered some light food and drink. We used flashlights sparingly for illumination. To use the toilet, we had to knock on the bottom of the trap door and ask to come up, one at a time. We were able to relieve ourselves, but always under constant pressure to hurry up and get back down into the dugout. Our hosts tapped their feet on the floor above us the next evening as a sign for us to finally gather our things and come up. Hiding our family was a brave gesture on their part. They took a huge risk since, if discovered hiding Jews, they faced immediate arrest.

My parents acknowledged their courage and kindness the best way they could every time they helped us hide. Anyu always made sweet treats for them. I remember my father calling the Šolc's and our other Christian friends very 'righteous people.'

Apu and Anyu carried a special white card at all times called a *Biale Karta*, a permit issued by the Slovak government that protected them due to their exceptional contribution to the city's commerce. On the days of the roundups, Dr. Šolc's sister, Maria, whose name was now officially listed with the city as the new proprietress of our store, would run the business all by herself. Once the round-ups came to an end however, namely when enough Jews were turned over to the Nazis to be transported to work in German factories, or so we were told, there would be an undetermined period of time until the next wave would occur. Then Anyu and Apu would be called to return to work. It could be days, weeks, or even months until the next round-up, and in the meantime, we had to lay low in the midst of constant and exhausting fear and uncertainty. To our dismay, the Jewish population of Prešov was visibly dwindling.

During a quiet time when the streets seemed safe, Anyu and I walked to our store. One day she ran into a friend, so we stopped and the two of them had a friendly conversation on the street. Without realizing it, Anyu carelessly made a critical remark about our mayor.

As it turned out, her comment might have been heard by any number of passers-by, no one knows for sure. Hearing them laugh, it appeared to me that both of them had a good chuckle and a fun time talking to each other. But the very next day a knock was heard on our door and two detectives came to arrest my Anyu. Poor Apu could do nothing about it. They took her away in handcuffs!

I was so scared about what might happen to her, I imagined the very worst. Apu felt terribly upset and helpless. When they arrested her, he wanted to know why they were taking her away. The answer was, "Your wife has insulted our honorable mayor in public. She will have to stand before the judge."

The police kept her in jail for two days and two nights. Apu, of course, notified his friend Judge Šolc who was able to lighten the severity of the case. After paying a fine, Anyu was released and allowed to return home. I was extremely happy to have her back. She was terribly shaken and didn't speak about her lockup at all. We never found out who snitched on her, but I was beginning to wonder who in the world we could trust.

During that winter we had a couple of big snowstorms. By then, at age seven and a half, I was big enough to sled by myself, so I convinced Apu to take me sledding on a Sunday morning on the steepest street in Prešov. Sunday is when all the stores were closed and hardly any traffic moved about. When we got there, the crowded street was teeming with kids pulling their wooden sleds and making all kinds of wild noises on the way down. I fell off my sled a few times but didn't get hurt. Apu always helped me pull the sled back uphill. It was the most fun I ever had. That day was a happy memory I will never forget.

Adolf Hitler
Photo: Bayerische Staatsbibliothek München/Bildarchiv

CHAPTER 8

The Round-ups Increase
1942

One morning in early March we heard an announcement on the radio, "All Jewish young women in Prešov between the ages of 16 to 34 are ordered by the Minister of the Interior, Mr. Alexander Mach, to report at eight o'clock in the morning on the following Wednesday to the main city square. Two suitcases with personal effects are allowed. Persons in non-compliance will be punished by the law."

Anyu told me that the young women were invited to travel to Germany to work in shoe factories with good paying jobs. This was in order to support the German war effort against the Communists. On March 25, 1942, the first transport of 325 unmarried Jewish women between the ages of 16 and 34, as specified, departed Prešov for the Poprad transit camp, a gated and heavily guarded detention camp. A few weeks later, some of my parents' friends whose daughters reported as ordered, told them that they had received postcards describing the good conditions in their working places and the nice treatment they were receiving at the hands of their managers. The women were also told they could return home eventually but, as far as we knew, none of them ever did.

Anyu assumed the happy reports were all a big lie. No one be-lieved the postcards, not for a minute. But no one was certain exactly what was going on. The following month, we learned that Jewish men between the ages of 16-34 from Prešov would also have to go to Germany to join the girls in the factories. By the end of the day on March 26th, 1000 women had been deported from Eastern Slovakia and actually sent to Auschwitz in Poland and by the end of April, a month later, over 1000 boys and men had been deported as well.

During this first wave of deportations, approximately 6,000 young, single Jewish Slovakian men and women from throughout greater Slovakia had all been deported to the labor camps in Germa-ny and Poland. But by that time, to our horror and disappointment, we learned that they had all been shamelessly coerced and deceived. News eventually filtered out that there were no shoe factories. It was all a lie. We further discovered that the cheerful postcards received by families had been written at gunpoint. It was unimaginable. The forced transfer of our finest young men and women was a hideous deception, soon to be followed by the taking of entire families, all in order to further Hitler's master plan, not yet known to any of us. And to think, our antisemitic Slovak Fascist government, completely dedicated to the *Führer*, facilitated all of it, along with the willful par-ticipation of some of our very own neighbors in Prešov.

As we sat around the radio listening to the BBC news, Uncle Tidi translated from English to Slovak. He told us about the war raging in Poland and in Russia. The German army was winning everywhere and had begun a major campaign to carry out the purging of Jews throughout Europe. My parents, grandparents, and Uncle Tidi were very sad and worried about what would happen to the Jewish people and our family. They said that we should have left before the war and joined Apu's family, the Štaubs and the Zieglers, who lived in America. There, they lived in peace.

Thank goodness, we didn't have war in Prešov. Not yet. We heard the sirens go off only once. We didn't go to the shelter; we stayed in our apartment. We didn't want to be seen by our neighbors. In spite of the white permit card, it would have been very dangerous since many informers snitched on Jews and got money from our government for turning them in. Anyu said it was an ugly and shameful thing.

My parents told me that it never used to be like this. People used to be friendly, it didn't matter what religion a person practiced. Now, even some of the Christians who were our friends before had become our enemies. They said that the Nazi government in Germany wanted to throw out all the Jewish people from Europe and that Adolf Hitler, *yimach shemo* (may his name be erased), said that we were not even humans. He called us enemies of his Reich. Sometimes, when he yelled in German on the radio, he called the Jewish people *untermenschen*, or subhumans. I didn't know what that meant exactly, but it couldn't have been anything good. He kept saying we Jews were the enemy that wanted to destroy Germany and all the rest of Europe.

Omama and Opapa grew terribly upset about the Nazi persecutions because they really liked the German language, books by German authors, and the music of German composer, Richard Wagner. They couldn't believe any of this was really happening.

"*Das ist nicht möglich!*" (It is not possible!) said Opapa in German, shaking his head. Omama agreed.

Due to the round-ups, I spent most of the summer indoors with the grown-ups, rarely going out. In a few months it would be fall and thereafter winter. I hoped the war would end quickly so I could go back to school and see my friends whom I missed. I also missed my cousins Irenka and Agì who lived in Trebišov, a city not too far away, and wondered how they were staying safe.

One memorable day, I looked out the window and saw a strange horse and buggy parked on the opposite side of the street in front of our building. A driver in a military uniform held the horse's reins. A few minutes later, my good friend Moishele, his little sister and his parents, came out of their building, forcefully pushed and shoved by two Hlinka Guardists. The parent's faces were ashen, and they were shaking. They threw their suitcases and some handbags on to the buggy and climbed in, sitting on their baggage and clutching the children tightly, with the two guards sitting on either side of them. Then the buggy left in a hurry.

I panicked and ran to the kitchen to tell Anyu what I had just seen. I was terrified. First she got angry with me for looking out onto the street. "Didn't I tell you to stay away from the window?" she scolded. "Someone may see you and call the Guardists." Then she told me that now they are taking whole families "to work" in Germany. Fear took further hold of me, and I wondered if that's where they were really going. Little Moishele and his sister were too young to work in a factory and his mother wasn't well. All I could think of was, "what if they come for us next?"

Hlinka Guard
© CTK – Photo 2022

Jewish women and children await selection on the ramp at Auschwitz-Birkenau.
Photo: United States Holocaust Memorial Museum courtesy of Yad Vashem.

CHAPTER 9

Trains with Human Cargo

In 1941, the Slovak government negotiated with Nazi Germany for the mass deportation of Jews to German-occupied Poland. Soon after, between March and October of 1942, some 58,000 Jews were deported to Auschwitz, the horrific concentration camp in the Lublin district of occupied Poland. The Jews throughout Slovakia grew even more terrified. The Slovak government actually organized these transports and paid 500 Reichsmarks, the currency used at the time, to Germany's Nazi-run government for each person displaced to cover the cost of "so called" resettlement (the payment of 500 Reichsmarks was equal to appx. $200 U.S. Dollars in 1942. Today that is the equivalent of appx. $3,500 U.S. Dollars per person). Many entire families were being "resettled" to Germany where they were told they would be given work assignments and their children would receive a good education. That was the official word from our Fascist government in Bratislava, but nothing made any sense.

The fall of 1942 had arrived and the skies grew dark earlier in the evening. Winter with its cold and heavy snows was clearly on its way. Meanwhile, our city of Prešov emptied of its Jewish citizens by the hour. Entire families seemed to disappear overnight. More frequently than before, Anyu took me with her wherever she went. One morning, she told me that we were getting on a train to Žilina in western Slovakia for some important meeting with family members. We were only going for one day. This was exciting news for me because I always loved riding on trains. To do so, Anyu needed a special permit to leave Prešov which took some time to arrange, but somehow, she succeeded. Once we were in the cabin of the train and on our way, Anyu explained to me that the real reason for our trip had to do with my Štaub grandparents and Anyu's beloved sister Rőszi Birnbaum and her family. But that was all she said.

The last time I had seen Rőszi *néni and* her husband Uncle Armin and my cousins Agi and Osi was at the Prešov train station just two days earlier. Anyu took me there because she was told they would be passing through. "Maybe we'll be able to talk to them while their train stops."

When the train arrived in Prešov station, we both had a big shock. There was a train alright. Parked on the first track was a long train made up of cattle cars with heavy, sliding doors guarded by several Hlinka Guardists with big guns. At first, we did not realize that the cattle cars were filled with passengers, Jewish passengers. When Anyu found out that the train came from Bardejov, where the Birnbaums lived, she immediately started to walk from car-to-car, calling out her sister's name. "Rőszi! Rőszi Birnbaum, Rőszi...!" Finally a voice responded from inside one of the cars. Incredible!

"Irén, Irén!" the voice called out.

At that point, my mother told me to stay where I was and walked over to a guard, starting a conversation with him. After a few minutes he looked around to see where the other guards were posted. Soon after, he quickly opened one of the sliding doors and the Birnbaums, barely visible amidst the packed crowd, started waving to us. The car was filled with people of all ages sitting on the floor and on suitcases, all crammed together. They looked helpless, fearful and exhausted. Anyu's sister shoved her way to the opening and she and Anyu had a fast conversation. Then the guard slammed the door shut. At that point, my mother started to cry, bitter tears streaming down her face, and I began to cry as well, right along with her. I didn't fully understand what I had seen or what was going on, but I felt terribly sorry for my two cousins and their parents. *Why were they there and why couldn't they be free?*

Anyu found out that the human cargo on the train was made up of Jews taken from towns all over Eastern Slovakia. The train was on its way to a temporary collection center in the town of Žilina, being used as a kind of holding place where Jews from various places and of different ages would be selected and redirected to labor or, as the world later learned, to extermination camps. Ironically, the people were offloaded and corralled like animals in Žilina's old Jewish cemetery, to be selectively redistributed onto other trains. Anyu was determined to go there; she would do anything to save her sister and my cousins.

Our passenger train trip took most of the day and we arrived in the afternoon. Upon arrival, we disembarked and went to search for our family. An armed guard stood at the entrance. Anyu was not intimidated. She instructed me to stand on the opposite side of the street, pretending she was alone. She and the guard had quite a lengthy discussion.

Suddenly, Anyu called for me to come fast. "Quick! We are going in!" She grabbed my hand and we both entered the cemetery. White tents were erected in-between the graves and hundreds of people were crowded in under the tents, a scene of controlled chaos. Hoping to get some information on how to find our relatives, Anyu entered the cemetery office. It didn't do any good. No one would speak to her or help us in any way. So, she and I walked from tent-to-tent, calling her sister's name until we found them.

"Roszi! Roszi Birnbaum!" we called out, over and over. Anyu's calls were answered at last and, upon finding each other, the two sisters hugged one another so hard I thought one of them would break. The meeting was bittersweet, much kissing, laughing and crying. Roszi and her children couldn't believe we had managed to come.

"Listen," explained Anyu to our cousins, "the purpose of my trip is to try and convince the government authority in charge to release you. I want to get you out of here before they send you away. This is our only chance."

My mother, still armed with the sacred white permit card arranged by Judge Šolc, spoke with her utmost authority and told the guards that she was taking full responsibility for returning our relatives to our home in Prešov where they would be cared for by us. But in spite of her best charm and most persuasive skills, she lost the battle. The guards refused. By the time we were ready to leave however, by sheer chance, we found our grandparents Omama and Opapa Štaub in the crowd! A miracle! Truly unimaginable. *Pán Božko*, the Slovak term for God, was surely looking out for us. We were filled with gratitude and joy. For some reason, the officers in charge did grant permission for my grandparents to leave with my mother and me. Their release was the greatest gift that day we could have imagined, and through our tears, we thanked God over and over for being able to save them.

We returned on the night train to Prešov. The trip was a partial victory. Omama and Opapa were back with us and safe, for now. After talking to them, we learned that Apu's youngest brother Tidi had left for Bratislava to be close to their sister, Ružena, who lived there with her husband Uncle Willy. They also told us that Apu's younger brother, Arnŏšt̆, had somehow succeeded in slipping out of Slovakia and was hiding in Budapest, the capital of Hungary.

Me with my mother of blessed memory,
Sarlota Irene (Grünfeld) Štaub, c. 1940

Collaborators Slovak interior minister Alexander Mach (left) and
German interior minister Wilhelm Frick (right). October 1942
Photo: public domain

CHAPTER 10

The Enemy in Our Midst

In December of 1942, just a few days before *Vianoce* (Christmas), I was playing with my favorite toys on the floor in what was once our store, a shop modeled after my paternal grandfather's similar business taken from us. Even under these difficult times, my parents were still allowed to work there and it was still known for beautiful, fashionable leather goods, gifts, fine musical instruments, records and exceptional, imported toys.

Customers bustled about since this was the busiest time of the year. At one point, I noticed a young German soldier who had entered the shop and was speaking to Anyu in German. I was too absorbed with my toys to listen closely, but I was fascinated. I'd never seen a German soldier up close before. I kept staring at his uniform with the silver buttons, broad black belt, and the bold, black and white swastika on his red armband. After looking at one of my toys closely for a few moments and buying something from my mother, he left.

Apu was gone when that exchange took place. Once he returned and began closing the shop, I returned all the toys to the shelves as I always did. It was then that I overheard Anyu telling Apu about this Wehrmacht soldier who had purchased a gift for his family earlier in the day. He told her he was passing through our city on his way from Poland to his own country.

"You cannot believe what happened Frici," said Anyu to Apu, anxious to tell him all that had transpired. "I was standing behind the counter when he came in. He just walked through the door like any other customer. It took my breath away! He walked around and checked the displays carefully, as if I wasn't even here. It made me so nervous. I watched him as he looked over the toy shelves and then the leather goods, until finally, he picked up a brown, Italian leather bag and brought it to the register."

"*Guten tag, Fraulein,*" he addressed me in German. (Good day.)

"Good afternoon, sir," I answered him. I could feel the color rise in my face. Beads of sweat dampened my forehead. "How can I help you?"

He didn't answer. He was watching Osi on the floor playing with a model German tank.

"Would you like this bag?" I asked, pointing to the handbag he set down before me. I could barely speak.

"*Ja, danke,*" (Yes, thank you.) he answered, eyeing me closely. Then he walked over to Osi and picked up the tank. "*Bitte?*" (Please?) He turned the toy around and upside down, examining the details. It was a miniature Panzer, made in Germany. He smiled, gave it back to Osi, and returned to the counter. "Can you wrap the bag?" he asked in German. "I am headed home to Germany for the holiday. It must make it all the way to Stuttgart."

"Of course," I said, my heart pounding furiously in my chest. Was he going to arrest us? Take us both away? Why didn't he just get it over with?

As I reached for the wrapping paper, I dared ask, "And where are you coming from?"

(Please forgive me, Frici. I don't know why I asked. God help me for even opening my mouth. I regretted it the minute I said it!").

Meanwhile, the soldier considered the question and answered, "I'm coming from the front, from Poland. You would not believe what I have seen and where I have been," he added, shaking his head somberly. "This war is a living hell."

He stared at the yellow Star of David sewn onto my blouse. "Jews are being killed and worked to death wherever you go. They are being wiped off the face of this continent." Then, looking straight into my eyes, he asked, "*Ist das dein kleiner junge?* " (Is this your little boy?)

"Yy-yes," I answered, stuttering. My hands gripped the counter. I hoped he couldn't see me trembling, but I was sure he could. I didn't know what was going to happen next.

Leaning over, closer to me, he lowered his voice and said, "*Ja fraulein*" (Yes, young lady*)*, you must be very careful. Do everything you can to save yourselves, *Verstehen sie?* (Do you understand?) "Don't let them take you away."

"And then, Frici, he put the package into his pack, patted Osi on the head, and left. The minute the door closed behind him, I took a deep breath and broke into tears."

Apu shook his head in disbelief. It meant the soldier knew exactly who we were, yet he protected us. Impossible, but it happened. In this strange time of roundups, deportations, terror and betrayal, it was a moment neither he nor Anyu would ever forget.

Jews were forced to wear a Jewish star stitched onto clothing.
Slovak stars stated *ZID* whereas stars in German read *Jude*.
Photo: Wayne Armstrong

In the days following the terrifying visit of the German soldier, Anyu
and Apu told all their close Jewish friends what took place.

"*Nemožne!*" they replied. (Impossible!) No one could imagine
such a thing! In order to stay safe from then on, my parents decided
to approach some of their Christian friends who could be trusted to
finally help us hide. Our closest non-Jewish friends were still Judge
Jozef and Margita Šolc. My father and Dr. Jozef had been friends in
high school. Apu later attended business school and expanded his
love of music while Jozef pursued law, eventually leading him to his
position of District Judge. Anyu and Margita liked each other and
often exchanged recipes for cakes, and sometimes went shopping to-

gether. Every year the Šolc's invited us to their home during Christmas to see their beautiful Christmas tree with the new decorations and celebrate their holiday with their children. They always had a gift for me under the tree.

Since coming to Prešov, Anyu had cultivated many friends, Jewish and otherwise. She had learned to play tennis, took cooking classes and liked to keep up with the latest fashions. All of these attributes and hobbies made her a very popular person. Apu did not have nearly as many friends, but between the two of them they had a busy social life and dear, trustworthy and generous Dr. Jozef and Margita Šolc were at the very center of it. We felt certain they would help us when the time came anyway that they could.

One night I heard Apu reading from the paper to Opapá whose eyesight wasn't so good anymore. Finding an objective newspaper back then was a rarity and a luxury. Most were filled with propaganda. But one column, written by a local reporter who was a member of the Nazi Party, caught Apu's eye. He read it aloud.

"Various political changes have been damaging to the relationships between Jewish and our mainly Christian communities. Some of the new laws aimed at separating the two religious groups have dire consequences if not observed strictly. Christians are no longer allowed to do business with Jews, or employ Jews, or vice-versa. Many old friendships have evaporated to the point of enmity. In some places, Christians have been forced to join the Hlinka Party for personal gain. Facism has taken the place of democracy, and tolerance and polarization of

the society have become the new order. Many Jews are being betrayed by former friends, understandably, and hiding them in any way is a crime against the state. It is strictly forbidden. Be aware, a few Christians have been punished for harboring Jews. Many more have openly become anti-Jewish, assisting in the process of cleansing our cities of the Jewish vermin. We must be vigilant and we must beware."

Apu put down the paper and looked at me apologetically, as if he'd forgotten I was there. This was not an article I should have heard. I stepped back, startled by his expression which was so solemn, it frightened me.

"Oskar, it is time for you to go to bed," he said. Then, turning to Opapá, added, "And it is time for us to get out of Prešov."

Time passed quickly and uncertainty mounted. One day in early 1943, Judge Šolc sent, as always, a warning to us before the round-ups. Under the cover of darkness, we always ran somewhere to hide. But more and more, we saw new fear and reluctance on the part of those who had previously taken us in to their homes. It had become too dangerous for them to continue.

"We were happy to help you before, but our neighbors have been suspecting us of hiding Jews," one neighbor said. "We are sorry, but they have been snooping around. We cannot help you anymore." This remark was a clear directive for Anyu and Apu to find an alternative hideout.

My parents, understandably, were mostly worried about me. I was just a little eight-year-old boy, and they were deeply concerned for my safety, for my future. They insisted it didn't matter so much what happened to them —they would manage. Anyu wanted to send me to her sister Ella and her husband Moric in Hungary to live with them until the war ended. They had two teenage daughters and Germany had not invaded that country yet.

"You'll have fun," Anyu assured me.

Panic took hold. I shook my head back and forth and cried, "No! No, no, no!" I couldn't believe my ears. I had never before been away from my parents. Leaving them was a terribly scary thought. "Please, don't send me away," I begged.

"Trust us, Osi," said Apu. "We know what's best. It's the only way. There is no future here."

"Please, please! Don't let me go anywhere without you!" Tears began to spill from my eyes.

"Oskar, we will not speak of it anymore," said Apu, more sternly than before. "We want you to be safe. And we have a plan. But first we have to find someone to smuggle you across the border."

Anyu put her arms around me and knelt by my side. "You trust me, don't you?" she asked softly, brushing away the tears rolling down my cheeks. "And you know we love you more than anything, right? Therefore, you will listen to us and you will do as you are told and be very brave about it." Then she put her finger to her lips as she often did, as if to tell me there was nothing more to say. Anyu always had the last word.

I stood there numb. I couldn't even process what they were saying. The words had no meaning, but they felt like a sharp knife in my young heart. Apu just stared at me with his sad eyes. I had a feeling that he would have rather had me stay.

My Anyu outfitted me with newly-purchased warm clothing prior to having me
professionally photographed in preparation for illegal crossing of the Hungarian border.
Prešov, March, 1943

CHAPTER 11

Crossing the Border
1943

My eighth birthday came and went in March of 1943. Shortly thereafter, Anyu took me to a children's clothing store to buy me a warm jacket, pants and sturdy boots, plus a hat and gloves for my upcoming trip. She took me to a photographer in my new outfit who snapped a couple of photographs. From there, she and I walked into a delicatessen. I will never forget her ordering a ham sandwich for me and telling me that, before my trip to Kassa, I would need a lot of energy. I reminded her that I shouldn't be eating *treif* (non-kosher food). She explained that, in our special circumstances, the saving of one's soul or *pikuach nefesh* in Hebrew, was of utmost importance and God would not punish me.

Sure enough, a couple of days later, a Christian man named Straka who worked in the local bakery came to pick me up. He knew the way to my Hungarian family in Kassa, a long day's walk from Prešov, just over twenty miles (32 kilometers). He was just one of many in the secret network of smugglers who helped Jews survive for a fee.

"You should not be afraid to go with him," Apu encouraged. "Mr.

Straka has crossed the border many times before successfully and has a friend, a border guard, who will arrange the crossing safely."

Anyu gave me a piece of paper before leaving our apartment. On it was written my Aunt Ella's last name and her address. She tucked it into one of my inside jacket pockets, but the idea that I was leaving made me too distraught to notice exactly where. Then she sat down, looked straight into my eyes, and said, "If a policeman were to stop you and ask where your parents are, do not tell him the truth. Make up stories. Tell him that your parents were killed by Nazis and you are an orphan."

This request puzzled me. My eyes grew wide as saucers as I stared back at my mother. Lie? To a grown-up? Then I started to cry and begged my parents again not to send me away. "I don't want to be an orphan!" I pleaded. "I don't want to lie! I want to stay, to be with you. I promise I won't cause any trouble."

"Osika, I told you that you will have a nice time with your Aunt Ella and your cousins," my mother countered. "They can hardly wait to see you. It will only be for a few weeks, until the war ends. Then you'll come back home to live with us again. I promise."

Anyu and Apu gave me kisses and hugs. Mr. Straka was asked to take my hand and leave with me in tow. No matter what, he was not to let go. The whole scene did not feel real. *This cannot be happening*, I said to myself. I was totally shaken, crying, and feeling sick inside. As we began to walk away, I looked back and caught a glimpse of my parents standing in the bedroom window of the small, courtyard cottage where we lived, fearing for our lives. My father 's face looked grim, his arms folded. My mother waved good-bye slowly and then turned away. I gripped Mr. Straka's hand even tighter and looked straight ahead, my vision blurred by a torrent of tears. After a while,

I felt completely numb, not even aware of where we were going.

As we headed away from the city, I became oblivious to the surroundings. Immense fear filled my entire body. I was beginning to mourn the loss of my dear Anyu and Apu as if they had actually been taken. The worst thoughts flooded my mind. Maybe the Hlinka Guardists had already come to pick them up and had taken them to the train station to be deported. Anyu was smart. She may have paid them money to wait until after I left. Maybe they were already gone. I didn't want to lose them— I loved them so much. They were my whole world.

Snow lay hard and frozen on the ground and my feet crunched over the crusty top layer while me and my smuggler walked. My face was chapped and cold and I could no longer feel my fingers. We continued to tramp through empty fields in the countryside, Mr. Straka first, with his heavy boots packing the snow, and me trailing slightly behind, still holding on tightly to his hand. It made my fingers hurt. Once in a while, he asked if I was tired and needed to rest or piss. He also told me that if we got separated, I should listen for his whistle. And if we ran in to anyone who asked, he would tell them that I was his son. "You be quiet," he instructed. "I'll do the talking."

After a while, the smuggler gave me water to drink and food to eat, but I was not so hungry. As we went, I saw snow covered pastures with cows, sheep and horses. Many dogs barked at us. They scared me, especially the big ones. In the countryside, wild dogs ran freely. In Prešov, the dog catchers captured stray dogs. I had seen them drive around and jump off the horse-drawn wagon chasing after a terrified dog with a large net. Sometime a big dog would attack them and try to bite. People stopped and watched the fight. Most of the time the dog catchers won. They locked the dogs in their wagons and drove away. I often wondered what happened to them, just like I wondered what was going to happen to us. I kept looking over my shoulder.

As we walked through the countryside, Mr. Straka told me that many stray animals are eaten by other wandering creatures such as wolves or foxes. At the same time, the peasants attack and kill the ones that are a threat to their sheep, chickens, goats, calves and domesticated pets. "The countryside could also be dangerous to people," he said, "especially at night." Thieves, bandits and runaway prisoners hid in forests and barns. *Žandáry*, (special police units) often conducted searches in villages, fields, and forests for criminals running from justice. "Walking through a village after dark could be life-threatening" he reminded, "especially for fugitives and strangers. Most peasants owned big, vicious guard dogs. Many owned hunting rifles as well and they didn't hesitate to use them if they felt threatened."

Mr. Straka left me completely terrified with all his scary stories and warnings. We couldn't get where we were going fast enough. But time passed slowly. In some places the snow lay knee-deep, yet we still had to struggle ahead. After many hours of trekking through the fields, I was chilled to the bone, my feet were drenched, my clothes were soaked and I was shivering. When I could not walk any further, my smuggler carried me on his shoulder. Every couple of miles he sat down on a log or a rock to rest for a few minutes. He kept telling me that by six o'clock, after it got dark, we would have to cross a creek before we reached the Hungarian border. If we were late getting there, we might not be able to get across at all. So, we pushed forward.

CHAPTER 12

Be A Rabbit

Finally, we reached the creek. Mr. Straka told me to sit down and be very quiet and not move an inch while he surveyed the area. I could hear water trickling in the half-frozen creek. I was completely exhausted, worried and scared. A few minutes passed in eerie silence. I heard distant voices floating through the crisp night air. It was hard to identify the language. Above our heads hung a full moon like a crystal ball with a scary face etched upon it. After a brief peek, I stopped looking. Throughout my entire childhood I had been warned by my grandmothers not to look into the face of the moon because it might pull me into it, or I might go mad like some of those people who ended up in the lunatic asylum.

Silently, my smuggler reappeared and took me to a place further down the creek where it was passable. He went in first and then helped me over. We crossed quickly without falling in or getting too wet. On the other side, we were staring at a wide, flat meadow covered with moonlit, silver-white snow. It looked like a pale, silken sheet reflecting the light from the moon in the dark night sky. The beautiful sight stretched from my far left to the far right, like a huge, magical painting. I felt hypnotized.

Mr. Straka told me in a whisper that I must cross the meadow alone. He pointed straight forward and told me to hunch down close to the snow and pretend to be a rabbit. He knelt beside me to show me the exact position. Then, I was to cross to the opposite side very quietly and carefully until I reached a distant stand of trees.

"When you reach them," he said, "sit down, rest, and wait for me. If you see someone or hear a noise, stop crawling, lay down flat, and wait until all is clear. If you hear me making an owl sound, a quick "hoot-hoot", lay down quick and wait until I whistle for you to continue."

I was more than scared, trembling all over. Mr. Straka gave me the signal to go. I crawled straight forward on my hands and knees. Luckily, I had warm gloves on. But after a while I felt my knees and fingers aching with the bitter cold. Then they went numb. I just kept pretending to be a bunny rabbit. My breathing grew heavy, but I followed a rhythm; arms and legs coordinated, left- right, left-right, following the beat of a song I liked, pretending I was dancing. Once I thought of Anyu, her beautiful smile.

Suddenly, I heard a distant pop, a loud sound like a rifle shot. Then a couple of men shouting something to each other and then, the hoot of an owl. I hit the snow flat on my stomach! Were these men hunting for rabbits? I could hear myself breathing hard, my heart beating like a drum. Then silence. Nothing moved. Straka whistled again, the sign for me to keep moving. I looked toward the trees. The more I stared at them, the more they looked like eerie human shapes, secretive and dark. What if there were soldiers in the trees waiting for me?

By then I was thoroughly soaked and numb all over from the cold and snow. At last, I reached the trees and realized that no one was there, no one was waiting. I sat down, shaking and shivering, but proud of my accomplishment. Still, I was too frightened to move. I took a deep breath. After a long while, Mr. Straka appeared and signaled, "Follow me. Once we get deeper into the forest we can stop to rest, eat and drink."

He circled my shoulder with his big gloved hand. "Good boy, Oskar," he said, using a normal speaking voice for the first time in hours. The sound of it startled me. He gave me a slight squeeze. "Now we are in Hungary."

CHAPTER 13

Interrogation

After a short rest, we emptied our bladders and continued our trek. "*Za dva hodiny už budeme tam,*" he said in Slovak. (In a couple of hours, we'll be there.)

"Be where?" I asked.

"You will see. Just keep walking."

All along I had been somewhat suspicious of him. I did not know him, nor did I fully trust him. At the same time, he was taking good care of me and doing his job. He gave me food and drink and now we had crossed the border to Hungary without being caught. I kept trying to calm myself and trust him more, especially these last few miles. He carried me on his shoulders most of the way until we reached a farmhouse. A big dog started barking as we approached the entrance and a peasant family welcomed us in. Plates with food awaited on the table, along with a pitcher of warm milk. We washed up, ate and drank, and I removed my wet boots. We were offered two low cots with blankets. I said a silent *shemah Yisrael* (a prayer in Hebrew and the first prayer I ever learned) and instantly fell asleep.

A woman's voice awakened me. "*Kis fijucska fel kel kelni!*" (Little boy, get up!) she said in Hungarian. I was confused and groggy and felt like I had barely slept. I washed, ate, and drank. The smuggler was gone. It was still quite dark outside. A strange man led me outside and told me to get into a small automobile. Gladly, I sat up front in the passenger seat. The driver started the engine, but after a few revolutions it quit running. The temperature was very cold inside the car and I was shivering. Finally, after a few attempts, the engine ignited and we were on our way.

I couldn't see much in the dark. Once in a while a tree or an electric pole zoomed by. The ride was noisy and uncomfortable, and the driver struggled to avoid potholes, swerving to the right and left and driving on a narrow dirt road. At one point, the ride became smoother thanks to pavement beneath our wheels. The sky grew brighter as dawn emerged and I could see the welcome shapes of houses and barns.

"We are almost in Kassa," announced the driver.

A few minutes later, I saw streets lined with large buildings on both sides. The car slowed down. The driver tried to read the names of the street signs. The sun was coming up by then and I was simply overwhelmed by the sights of this beautiful city, with its broad streets and tall, elegant buildings. Following a series of right and left turns, the driver stopped the car abruptly on a street corner. He told me to get out and wait for my family on the sidewalk. That was it. Goodbye.

I got out and looked around. The street was empty. Behind me, I saw a big church and a park void of people. It was early morning, and the stores were still closed. A noisy streetcar rolled by a few feet away on the adjacent street. *It must be the main street*, I thought to myself. *Maybe I should go there.* As I waited for someone to show up, I started to shiver again from the cold and began to feel very scared to be in a strange city all by myself. *What if Aunt Ella forgets to pick me up?* I began to panic and tears filled my eyes. I was alone and lost. How would I find my family?

A man approached. Could it be Moric? On second glance, I realized he was a policeman. He asked me in Hungarian "*Hogy hivnak téged?*" (What is your name little boy?) "Are you waiting for someone?"

"Oskar," I replied, "and yes, I am waiting for my Aunt Ella."

"Where are your parents?"

"I don't have parents. I am an orphan," I answered, hanging my head. I swallowed hard. My eyes were brimming with tears.

"*Hol születtel?*" (Where were you born?)

"*Eperjesen,*" (In Prešov.) I answered.

"*Te tudod hol lakik Ella néni?*" (Do you know where your Aunt Ella lives?)

"*Nem.*" (No.)

"I can't let you stand here alone, Oskar," he continued in Hungarian. "Come, let's go to the police station. It's nice and warm there. We'll try to find your aunt."

I was terrified. I wanted my parents. I felt like crying. But quietly, I followed the policeman. I could have run away, but he would have chased after me. And where would I have gone? *Pán Božko drahý* (my dear Lord God), *please don't let the policeman hurt me. I should have not agreed to come here. I should have stayed with Anyu and Apu.* As I walked, I wiped away more tears on my cold, damp sleeve, fearful of the unknown.

The sign on the two-story, red brick building read: *CSENDÖRSÉG.* (Police.) I followed the policeman up the steps to the second floor into an office. He moved a chair into the middle facing a large desk, told me to sit down, and left. Then, another person came in with a large bowl filled with water which he placed on a chair to my right. He lay a towel on the chair. "Be patient little boy. Soon officer Csatáry will come talk to you."

Time passed very slowly. I was glued to the chair, afraid to get up. Scary thoughts ran through my mind. I was growing more fearful by the minute, my insides shaking.

A large clock on the wall told me that over an hour had passed since I arrived. Finally, the door opened and in came a short, chubby police officer. He sat behind the desk, placed his revolver upon it, adjusted his chair and looked straight at me. He did not smile. I could not take my eyes off that revolver—it was big and shiny and threatening. I felt nervous just looking at it.

Next, he began to interrogate me in Hungarian, one intrusive question after another. "What is your name? How old are you? Where were you born?" He continued with even more. "Where are your parents? Where did you learn to speak Hungarian? How did you get here?"

Remembering what my Anyu and Apu told me, I answered each question, carefully making sure I didn't falter, all the while staring at the gun on the table. "I am an orphan," I explained. "My parents, who taught me to speak Hungarian, were taken away by Nazis. My Anyuka told me to run to my Aunt Ella in Kassa while she and my father were being dragged away by the mean soldiers. Then they were shot."

By now I was crying from fatigue, fear, and being forced to lie. The stress was overwhelming. The officer stopped questioning me, told me to relax, and left. A lady entered the room, brought water and crackers, and told me where the toilet was if I needed to use it.

After a while, I stopped shaking and regained my composure. By mid-day, the same lady brought more food, along with words of consolation. I think she felt sorry for me. Shortly after finishing eating, a man came in dressed in civilian clothes. He smiled and said cheerfully, "Come along young man. We are going for a ride. I will show you the city. Don't be afraid."And so, for the next hour and a half, I sat in the passenger seat next to a detective being questioned again and again as he showed me the different parts of Kassa, asking me to show him the direction I came from. "Did anyone show you the way? Was that person from Slovakia or was he Hungarian?"

Of course, I continued my lies and told him that I walked on my own for several days, stopping to sleep in farmhouses where they gave me food and water and showed me which way to walk to Kassa. I also got a couple of rides from friendly peasants. As I promised Anyu, I kept the truth to myself.

When the plainclothes detective realized that he couldn't get any information from me, frustrated, he drove us back to the police headquarters. My fear of being beaten up, although real, never happened. Both of my interrogators tried to lead me to the smugglers, alternating threats with kindness, to no avail. In the late afternoon, officer Csatáry asked me, "Do you have family living here in Kassa?"

"Yes!"was my answer.

"What is their name?"

Suddenly, I remembered the paper in my pocket. But which pocket? Where did Anyu put it? There, I found it and gave it to the officer. He saw their names, Ella and Moric Zinger. He picked up the phone and dialed their phone number which he found in the town directory. Someone answered and about a half an hour later Aunt Ella and her daughter Judit showed up to claim me. As I was being released, Officer Csatáry made Aunt Ella sign a legal form saying that she took full responsibility for my well-being as an orphan. And I signed a form which required me to report to him every second Friday, which I did religiously.

A great relief cured my apprehension when my relatives claimed me, hugging and kissing me upon my release from the police station. Pride and joy replaced fear and sadness as I began a new life with my loving family. The warm welcome I received restored my sense of well-being. I felt safe at last A good meal, a warm bath and a good night's sleep were a well-earned reward following a thirty-six-hour, terrifying journey.

Aunt Ella and Uncle Moric Zinger with granddaughter Eva Lysy.
c. 1949

CHAPTER 14

Life with the Zinger family
in Kassa, Hungary

The Zingers lived a comfortable life on Farangos Street, a couple blocks away from the reform Neolog synagogue. The spacious three-bedroom apartment on the ground floor accommodated a family of six, including me. Located only six miles from the Slovak/Hungarian border, it was like another world. Life for Jews in Kassa was noticeably better. The Nazis had not yet come to Kassa and Jewish people were not forced to be identified by wearing yellow stars on their clothing. They still were free to have jobs and work.

Grandma Grünfeld (my mother and Aunt Ella's mother), sometimes called *nagy-mama*, also lived there. She had her own bedroom, but during the day would sit and often pray in the living room. Once in a while Aunt Ella would take her shopping. Grandma and I did not see eye-to-eye. She was superstitious and demanding. Like all religiously observant Orthodox Jewish women, her hair was always covered with a kerchief, except on Friday night and Saturday when she attended religious services in the Orthodox synagogue and wore a wig. She mostly wore long, dark clothing and looked at me sternly whenever she was disturbed by my behavior. I avoided her.

Once-a-week a nurse came to the apartment with a jar of leeches which she placed on grandma's back. The black slimy things barely moved as they sucked her blood. This treatment was prescribed by her physician to control her blood pressure. When this happened, I couldn't stand being around. I preferred to go out and play with my new friends in the courtyard.

During the week, I attended the third grade at a Hungarian public school. I enjoyed learning how to read and write. After school I did my homework. Dinner was served at six o'clock, promptly! Aunt Ella cooked up good meals. I was the happiest when my two cousins Judit (15) and Rŏszi (17) came home from school. They treated me like their little brother. The three of us had a common connection, the love of music. Rŏszi played the piano and Judit loved to sing. On the weekends they taught me Hungarian songs, dances and stage-craft. They teamed me up with Nadja, a talented ten- year-old Jewish girl who lived on the second floor above us.

Nadja was too serious for me and therefore, I was not very fun to be around. But, as it was said, even in Slovak, "the show must go on," so reluctantly, I continued to rehearse dance routines and learn the music and lyrics to current popular songs with her. I got used to holding her hands and putting my hand around her waist as we worked out tap dance routines, something my father taught me how to do, and harmonized. As a rule, I didn't favor girls with glasses and Nadja wore them due to her poor vision. As time passed however, and we began to entertain adults and children of all ages, we relaxed with each other and became friends.

Some months earlier we were entertaining in the Jewish orphanage. After the program, two girls came to compliment me and I recognized them. They were my cousins Irena and Agi, the daughters of Uncle Jenö and Aunt Teréz from Trebišov in Slovakia. We were hugging and kissing, happy to see each other. They arrived in Kassa a couple of weeks after I did. Mr. Straka, the smuggler, brought them over the border, too. Aunt Ella invited them to stay with us as well, but due to lack of space in her apartment, they ended up living in the Jewish orphanage. I was excited to have them here.

Irena was my favorite cousin. Beautiful, soft-spoken and well-mannered, I loved her like a sister. Her sister Agi, on the other hand, was a troublemaker. She was loud, rude, and always interrupted when I talked to her sister. She annoyed me. The last time she visited us in Prešov, Anyu made her sleep in my bed and all she wanted was to see my private parts and ask me all kinds of questions about how babies were born. It didn't matter. Seeing them helped me with my loneliness.

In the fall of 1943, I was invited by the choir master of the nearby Neolog synagogue to audition for the all-male choir just before the High Holy Days, two Jewish holidays that are always celebrated in the fall. Apparently, they followed the tradition of not mixing male and female voices. My voice back then was high and clear. When I finished singing one of the Hungarian songs for them, they all applauded. I was the youngest choir member. The older boys sang second and third parts; I sang the melody. After services on both holidays, Rosh Hashana, the Jewish New Year, and Yom Kippur, the Day of Atonement, many adults complimented me.

This recognition only meant that my family would get even more requests for me and my partner to entertain. We were always glad to do so. On certain Sundays, I was given a special treat by the Zinger family. They had subscription, season tickets to the Hungarian National Theater. About once-a- month they took me along to see an operetta by world-renowned composers such as Offenbach, Lehar, Kalman and others. I could hardly wait to walk into the beautiful theater and get lost in the wonderful magic of music. Every time we sat in the same box or loge on the upper right-hand side where we had an excellent view. The leading roles were played and sung by famous performers, stars of the Budapest National Theater. My cousins informed me that they were trying to arrange an audition for me with the theater's artistic director. The very idea thrilled me. Performing on that stage was beyond anything I could have hoped for.

Dancing with my partner, Nadjia Maigtin.
Kassa, Hungary, 1943-44

Oskar Štaub
Kassa (Kosice), 1943

CHAPTER 15

My Musical Debut

One day after school was out, Judit picked me up and we walked to the theater. There, the artistic director, a man with long hair and a bright red scarf, showed me the way to a rehearsal room. "Osika, sing and dance for me please," he asked.

Judit suggested I perform my routine to the tune of some the very popular songs of the day. So I sang and tap danced, accompanied by the piano. I was super excited and nervous. If he liked me I would be appearing in a spring musical. Wow! When I was done, he declared with a broad smile, "I've been looking for a talented kid like yourself. We'll start rehearsing in late January or early February."

On our way out he told Judit, "I'll call you with the rehearsal schedule next month." He shook my hand and expressed his satisfaction at finding me. I was elated. This was a dream come true.

Nadja and I had been invited to perform at the community holiday banquet in preparation for the Festival of Chanukah. We rehearsed almost daily. The dinner and celebration were typically attended by over 500 people. Our program consisted of two Hungarian songs: *"Szerelemhez Nem Kel Szépség"* (To Be in Love, You Don't Need Beauty) and *"Kelemen Maga a Multam és a Jelenem"* (Kelemen, You Are My Past and My Present). We worked on dance routines and some harmonizing. Judit also sang some solos. Judit, the vocalist and Rŏszi , my talented accompanist, were tough taskmasters.

The program was a smash hit and followed by long audience applause. My cousins were proud of me and proud of themselves and Rŏszi made a great accompanist. Following that performance, I continued to wait patiently for the rehearsal notification from the National Theatre, counting the days.

(L-R) Nadia Maigtin, my cousins Rozsi and Judith and myself
- dressed in costume - as I was performing in a *Operetia* production.
A Chanukah Jewish community event in Kassa, Hungary 1943

In the meantime, school vacation ended. The celebration of *Silvester* or New Year's Eve passed, and the calendar now read January, 1944. So far, no word had arrived from the theater. Every once in a while, someone conveyed greetings from my parents, delivered by smugglers who came from Prešov. Those were my happiest moments. They gave me hope that I might see Apu and Anyu again sometime soon. I never stopped thinking about them or wondering if they were alright.

As time went on, I played a lot with my new friends in our apartment complex. About a dozen family dwellings on two floors faced the courtyard where we gathered. Besides Nadia, there were four girls and two boys my age. Our favorite games were hide n' seek, hopscotch, and various combination games with colored marbles. Before Christmas, the chestnut vendors set up their businesses all along the main street nearby. The wonderful aroma reminded me of winters in Prešov with my parents. Aunt Ella occasionally braved the cold and walked me down the block to get a treat.

About once a month, Uncle Moric allowed me to go with him to his flour mill in Barca. He hitched his horse to a two-wheeled carriage called a cabriolet and we trotted merrily along on the narrow country road. The trip lasted a little under an hour. When he wanted to be nice, he handed over the reins and showed me how to use the whip if the horse got lazy and slowed down. I seldom used it. I didn't like to hurt the horse.

The mill had been built on a large parcel of land. It became my playground. The building stood three stories high, with steps going in all directions, and wherever you looked, you saw huge piles of sacks filled with flour. Big wheels with conveyor belts created a great deal of noise. It was a place of mystery and fun. When I got my fill of climbing inside the mill, I climbed a fence into a vast orchard of assorted fruit trees and proceeded to climb them and eat the ripened fruit. On a couple of occasions, Uncle Moric allowed me to bring a friend but curtailed the activities inside the mill. He preferred that we play in the orchard.

"Be careful children, don't hurt yourselves climbing trees," he warned as we ran to the fence. At the end of the day, we used the caretaker's house to wash up and change clothes before heading back home. Going to the mill was by far my new favorite pastime.

CHAPTER 16

An Orthodox Life and
My First Crush

The Zinger family mostly favored indoor activities. That was the case with most Orthodox Jews. Life focused on family, close friends, synagogue, and the study of Torah. Besides pursuing their high school education and their musical interests, my cousins Rőszi and Judit were not outdoorsy persons. Beginning on Friday, everything switched into Shabbos (the Sabbath) mode; namely a maid came in to prepare the house by dusting, cleaning, washing floors and helping Aunt Ella with cooking and the usual pre-Shabbat chores. Uncle Moric took his weekly bath and assumed his role as the supreme leader of the family.

Following the lighting of candles by the women, Uncle Moric sat down at the head of the table to read a passage from the scripture and the portion of the week. He had me wash my hands with him and say the *bracha* or blessing in Hebrew "*Al netilat yadayim,*" (washing of the hands). Following the recitation of the Kiddush, or sanctification of the Sabbath, the women scrambled to serve the meal. Food was always plentiful.

Aunt Ella prepared great meals, being a very good cook. But the chicken soup here also had circles of fat floating on top, which I disliked. I did not dare complain especially since I always sat to the right of Uncle Moric and didn't want to get smacked. The rules of observing the Sabbath were strictly kept. The time was one of rest and reflection, relaxation and prayer. Work was forbidden. Neither lights nor flame were to be turned on or off for twenty-four hours. The non-Jewish maid did all the work enabling us to maintain our traditions. If she was not around, the Shabbat *goy*, a non-Jew who lived nearby, was summoned to help. Even the phone was disconnected.

Saturday mornings, all six of us rose early, put on our nice clothes, and followed Uncle Moric to the Orthodox synagogue for Shabbat services. The ladies sat upstairs and I, of course, had to sit with the head of the household downstairs with all the men. Every few minutes Uncle Moric glanced at my prayer book to make sure I was on the right page. I didn't know how to read Hebrew yet, but that didn't matter. Like a little monkey, I did what the congregation did. I took my directions from my strict uncle. "Stand up. Sit down. Sit down. Stand up. You may go now outside to play with your friends but come back in fifteen minutes." In the meantime, I went upstairs to visit the ladies. I had more fun there. Many of them knew me and motioned for me to come over. My *nagymama* (grandmother) took prayer very seriously. So did Aunt Ella.

Röszi and Judit liked to socialize. One of them usually joined me when I went outside to play with my friends. Services were boring so I stayed out as long as possible and always returned late. During the last High Holy Days services, I was really bored, especially on Yom Kippur. We spent an entire, very long day in services. I had to fast until mid-afternoon when the congregation took a break. My cousins and I walked back home. There they fed me a snack of *lekváros kenyér* (bread with jam) and a drink. The best part of Yom Kippur was always the break-the-fast meal, served after the sun went down. I liked most of the foods served such as herring, also *kuchen* (cake), *kakaoš* (chocolate roll), *makoš* (poppy seed strudel), *dijoš* (nut cake), *kugel* (noodle pudding), and many other delicious foods.

Of all the holidays, however, I preferred Sukkot, another Jewish fall celebration. I helped decorate the *sukkah* that the Zingers built, a little hut open on three sides with a roof made of palm branches imported from Israel through which you could see the sky. The hut is supposed to remind us of the tents our Biblical forefathers erected when they were out gathering the harvest in the fields for many days. According to tradition, we ate all our meals in the sukkah for one full week.

To wait for news from the theater's artistic director was nerve wracking. Chanukah had come and gone and I was still waiting to hear about rehearsals. What kept me happy those days was my new girlfriend Éva who went to my school. I found her very pretty, but also very shy. I tried to talk to her but she seldom answered. Sometimes I stared at her during class. When she looked at me, I quickly turned my head in the other direction. Finally, I decided to take flowers to her for her birthday. My cousin Judit told me where she lived.

I trembled as I walked up to her door, gathering all the nerve I had in my eight-year-old body. I held the bouquet in one hand and knocked with the other. The door opened. I expected to see Évike (an endearment for Éva), but instead her mother towered over me.

"May I help you, little boy?" she asked.

'I want to speak to Évike, please," I stuttered, feeling like I was sinking into the ground.

"She is busy now. Come back later."

The plan was failing. I couldn't come back later. "I would like to wish her a happy birthday," I said. I felt so embarrassed.

Her mother reached for the flowers. "I will give her these," she said. She took the flowers from my hand and began to close the door. I was about to cry.

"Please, tell her that Osi brought them."

"I will tell her."

The door closed suddenly, and I couldn't move. I just stood there petrified. I felt so stupid. I hated Eva! I hated her mother. I hated myself. Strange feelings and emotions raced through me. How could I be so dumb? My day was ruined. The next day I pretended she was not even in class. It would have been nice if she had thanked me for the flowers at least. I felt so disappointed. But the days passed by and after a while, I grew calmer. I decided to say hi to her. She walked by me and gave me a little smile. Maybe I still liked her. I hoped that someday she might talk to me.

Shortly after this discouraging incident, I was walking home one Sabbath afternoon wearing my good Shabbat clothes; a woolen suit with a nice jacket, pants and a hat. The route required passing by the local public swimming pool. I had never learned to swim, and I watched the swimmers enviously as I approached. But suddenly, out of nowhere, I was pushed forward with a sharp shove, and fell straight into the water in the deep end! I sank immediately, weighted down by my soggy clothes, then somehow floated back up, terrified and screaming for help when I reached the top. Sputtering and flailing around, someone finally rescued me. I'll never know who. I only know I made it home, still terrified and soaking wet, having come close to drowning on that unforgettable and humiliating day. I was reluctant to go out in Kassa by myself after that.

CHAPTER 17

The War Closes In and Hungary Betrays Its Jews 1944

One disappointment led to another. Judit told me that she called the theater and inquired about the starting date of the rehearsals for the next musical. Instead of the director picking up the phone, his secretary did. It seems that they found another child actor who was more suitable for the role. That was it. This news left a more devastating blow than the flower delivery episode with Eva. I could not understand. I thought they liked me. For a number of days, I was very depressed. I didn't feel like talking to anyone or eating anything. What had changed?

After school, I often checked to see if my lieutenant friend was at home. He lived on the second floor, a couple of doors away from Nadja's apartment. He served in the *huszar* (cavalry), a regiment of the *Magyar* (Hungarian) military. A nice man, much younger than my parents, he let me polish his long, steel sword and, once a week, his tall black boots as well. He was my hero, especially when he wore his ceremonial uniform with all the special insignias and medals.

He said he liked having me around and I liked hearing his military stories.

I really liked going to school in Kassa. Now, in addition to speaking Hungarian much better than when I arrived, I read storybooks and could also write and spell words correctly. My teacher was impressed with my progress. My marks were good and my family was proud of me.

I had been paying more attention to the news on the radio, however. The news was terrifying. The German army boasted of victory on all fronts. Thousands of soldiers were dying in Europe and further south, no one could stop the advance of the mighty Panzers under the command of General Erwin Rommel in North Africa. The Nazis were everywhere. In addition, horrible stories about mass killings of Jewish people in Poland circulated in the Jewish community. Whole towns had been decimated. We heard many discussions regarding the safety of the Jews of Hungary.

The adults around me discussed all kinds of ideas about the political situation and the ability of Regent Miklos Horthy (the leader of the national government in Budapest) to withstand the pressure coming from members of the government, eager to collaborate with the German military occupation authorities. My family said over and over that they had complete confidence in the strength of Regent Horthy to protect the Hungarian Jewish community from persecution. But I could sense a certain tension among them and I didn't believe what they said.

One day, my Uncle Moric asked me to join him. "Come Osika, I need your help." I knew better than to ask for an explanation, so I simply followed him. He carried a shovel and a box. We went down to the lowest level of the building to the storage rooms. In one of them, I saw a large area divided by a kind of low fencing.

"Shhh," said my uncle. "We must be very careful. Keep your voice down."

I watched while he dug a hole in the dirt floor and inserted a metal safe-box filled with the family's personal belongings and some important documents. While he dug, I was to look out and act as a guard in case anyone might enter the area. Until he finished, I realized I was holding my breath.

As time passed, I heard arguments and disagreements at home almost every day. The phone rang more frequently, followed by whispered conversations. Aunt Ella and her husband were obviously trying to protect me and my grandmother from hearing the latest bad news. Every once in a while, when a heated debate occurred between my cousins and their parents regarding the future of our community, I could hear Aunt Ella say in Hungarian, "*A gyerek itt van.*" (The child is here; tone it down.)

Each day brought more change and uncertainty. The nights were the worst. Ever since I arrived, after Aunt Ella tucked me in, I secretly cried myself to sleep, missing my parents so much and wishing I was home. Between my sobs, I wondered if they had been rounded up while I was gone, or were even still alive, and if they were, if they were missing me, too. Some nights I had terrible nightmares and would wake up in a panic, dreaming that I was lost.

Of late, I had begun to worry about my own safety, a gnawing, heartsick feeling of anxiety. I sensed in my gut the coming of serious trouble. I did not want to get trapped in Hungary if the country were to be invaded by the German army. Besides, I felt a deep and fierce longing for my parents who I desperately wanted to be with again. We needed to be together. I was told they were still surviving safely in Prešov and I knew I had to get back to them before things got worse. I dared not get caught in a Nazi military takeover in Kassa. I did not know why, but my family here seemed unresponsive to what others sensed was the oncoming devastation. The signals were everywhere. I no longer trusted Aunt Ella and Uncle Moric to look out for me.

Dark clouds gathered over Kassa. Day-by-day, I became less focused on school and my circle of friends. I could not concentrate. At night I had trouble falling asleep, and awoke more and more often, fearful of something unnamed and unknown. All the good feelings I enjoyed during my pleasant life in Kassa when I first arrived —the calm, the joys of childhood, the reassurance of family and the warm feeling of security, were now overshadowed by the frightening developments surging around us. I might have been just a child, but I could sense the danger and feel the evil threat of Nazi Germany. It felt like a piece of ice freezing in my heart, like cold water running through my veins.

CHAPTER 18

The German Invasion
March 19, 1944

We celebrated my ninth birthday with cake, ice cream and birthday candles, plus the presence of Irena, Agi, Nadja, Évike, (still friends even after the flower incident) and my friends in the complex. We enjoyed a fun party. The next day, as usual, the radio was on in the morning which was appreciated, since here, they were not illegal. As I rushed to get ready to go to school, a news broadcast caught my attention.

"At noon today, officers of the local cavalry, together with the leaders of our municipality, will welcome a division of the distinguished German army to our city. The brief ceremony will be held on Petöfi Square. Citizens are invited to attend and help us welcome our German friends."

I said goodbye, kissed Aunt Ella, and headed out the door. I got to school a few minutes late. My teacher commented on my being tardy. I had been tardy before, so I ignored her.

"Tomorrow you will bring a note from your aunt," demanded my teacher. She was not pleased. The morning passed very slowly. All I wanted to do was get to the square by noon to see the welcoming of the German army. I felt nervous, curious, and scared. At half-past eleven, I began to fake a stomachache. My hand went up.

"What is it?" said my teacher.

I replied, "I have a bad stomachache. I feel nauseous. May I please go to the restroom?"

On my way out of the classroom, she said in Hungarian, "If you are sick, go home." Then she added, "Tomorrow, as I said, you will bring a note from your aunt." My classmates told me to feel better. A couple of troublemakers laughed out loud and said I was faking it.

I walked fast and headed straight to the plaza. A crowd of adults were already lined up on both sides. My insides trembled. I did not want to be seen and tried to be very small. I sat down on the edge of the sidewalk amidst the crowd and looked between people's legs. On the right was a cluster of beautiful white horses mounted by Hungarian officers who were dressed in fancy, colorful uniforms. The horses were restless, moving sideways and tossing their heads. The riders struggled to control them. A few minutes passed and the crowd shifted its gaze to the left. First, I heard the rumble of an engine and soon, a long, green convertible appeared heading towards the center of the plaza, followed by trucks filled with German soldiers. Other types of vehicles entered behind the lead cars. Then they all stopped. Two officers stepped out of the lead car. Someone near me whistled and said, "It's a Mercedes!" I had never seen a luxury car like this, with a huge chrome grill in front, and long, curved fender caps, plus a leather hard-top that rolled down to the back seat. There, inside, several German officers stood, waving to the crowd.

The whole scene seemed unreal and awe-inspiring. At the same time, something was amiss in the way the Hungarian officers looked compared to their German counterparts. The German uniforms were a formal, light bluish-gray, as were their snappy, neat fabric hats, trimmed with shiny, black brims. Menacing revolvers hung from their black leather belts. They wore medium-height, black boots, highly polished.

The Hungarian uniforms, by contrast, looked like parade costumes; crimson-red jodhpurs for riding horses, knee-high, black riding boots, green jackets, cross-body, leather strap pouches hanging from their shoulders, and long swords in shiny sheaths attached to wide, black belts. On their heads they wore grey caps with short, white feathered plumes pointing upward. The Hungarians almost looked comical while the Germans looked neat, efficient and threatening.

The two groups came together and shook hands. I wondered if they understood each other's language. A small group of civilians led by the mayor of Kassa also welcomed the German officers, marking the beginning of a major military collaboration. Their conversation was not audible to me because of the distance. Besides, the onlookers were all talking to each other as well. I didn't stay long and left feeling very agitated. Uncontrollable fear once more entered my heart and brain.

As I slowly walked home, my head began to swirl with all kinds of worried thoughts. *What will happen to us now that the Germans are here? What would Anyu and Apu want me to do? All I know is, I must find a way out of Kassa.* My eyes were filling up with tears. During dinner that night I heard no mention of the day's events. Finally, but with some hesitation and risking a reprimand for skipping school, I asked my aunt and uncle if they were aware of the German army's presence in our city.

"Aren't you worried?" I asked.

Quizzical faces turned my way. Aunt Ella and Uncle Moric shook their heads, indicating "No, they were not worried." Their answer upset me. They basically shrugged their shoulders and expressed their total faith in the Hungarian government's commitment to protect the safety of the Jewish population.

"Regent Miklós Horthy will not let the Germans touch us," said Uncle Moric and gave me a weak smile. I wondered if he believed it. "Besides, we are fully entitled citizens with a long history in *Magyar Ország* (the country of Hungary). The Jewish people have contributed greatly to the strength of our economy, industry, finance, and even culture. Don't worry, Osika, you are safe here."

"Well, I don't feel safe anymore," I replied. "I think we should make plans to leave, or move to another city where people don't know our background," I continued in my most adult voice. "We should find a hiding place in case the authorities begin the roundups of Jews here."

My comment fell flat. No one said a word. I guess it didn't matter what I thought. I was just a little boy, so I retreated knowing that I was right and they were foolish. But that night I could not fall asleep. The parade in the square kept replaying in my brain. My feelings and emotions rolled back to what they were saying and what was happening in Prešov, before I was smuggled to my family here in Kassa. My gut was telling me to get out. I had to send a message to my parents right away.

My frustration with my family's lack of concern angered me. Within a few days, I became increasingly mischievous and at times, arrogant. I lost patience with my friends. In school, I couldn't concentrate on my studies. My mind was preoccupied with ideas of escape in case of a Nazi roundup, and I preferred to be alone. I started teasing a small cat and repeatedly tried to puncture the postman's bicycle tires. One morning, I was able to drive a thick, heavy needle deep into the back tire. When the postman was done distributing the mail, he jumped on his bike only to discover that the back tire was totally flat. I quickly ran into our apartment and hid under a bed. The angry postman must have seen me running. He entered our flat and carried on like a lunatic, screaming and waving his arms, demanding that I appear. He wanted to kill me.

Aunt Ella protected me. She calmed him down promising him that I would be sorely punished. "He will never touch your bike again." The postman left and I emerged from under the bed. I told my aunt that very day that, unless I could return to my parents, I would cause more trouble. I just couldn't help myself.

Saturday night, after the *havdalah* ceremony celebrating the end of the Sabbath and the start of a new week conducted by Uncle Moric, Omama made me so angry that I grabbed one of her spare wigs and threatened to throw it into the fireplace. I scared the wits out of her. She started to scream as if she was in pain. "*Ooy, ooy, ooy*, my wig, my wig! What has happened to this sweet little boy? He is turning into a devil!"

CHAPTER 19

I Must Return to Prešov
April 1944

Over and over, I expressed my demand to be returned to my parents. My erratic behavior continued from the time the German army was welcomed to Kassa until one memorable day in the middle of April when my prayers were magically answered. A stranger knocked on the door saying that he had been sent by Mr. & Mrs. Frici Štaub to take their young boy, meaning me, Osika, back to Prešov!

I got all excited listening to him speak to Aunt Ella. But his arrival came as a total surprise. No one told me about him coming. Obviously, she must have been in touch with Anyu. It might have resulted from my outburst at the dinner table a few nights earlier. I threatened, "If you don't arrange for a smuggler to take me back to my parents, and soon, I will run away on my own, and if something terrible happens to me, my mother will never forgive you."

Somehow, Aunt Ella must have gotten word to her. I learned later that to get messages across the border, some people actually sewed a note into a person's clothing by inserting it into the padding in the shoulders of a jacket or coat so it was invisible. I assume that is what

Aunt Ella did. But I will never know for sure.

I joined my aunt at the door and looked up to see a very tall, lanky man wearing a long, smelly black coat with a black patch over one eye, and sporting a long scar on his left cheek. He looked like a pirate, right out of a storybook I once read —a scary-looking monster. *What to do now?* I walked up and down the courtyard, totally confused. I changed my mind several times; *Should I or shouldn't I go with him? Should I even go at all?* Finally, I calmed myself. I had to trust my mother's reason for hiring this particular man to take me back to Prešov. She loved me too much to risk my safety. *Dear God,* I prayed, *protect me from harm if I decide to go with him. Then again, what choice did I have?*

And so, on a rainy April morning, my pirate came back for me. I put on my warmest clothes and the same boots I wore last year which still fit me. Aunt Ella kept hugging and kissing me and crying bitterly. I said goodbye to everyone. A faint feeling of anxiety washed over me that felt for a moment like regret. *Maybe I shouldn't go,* I thought again. *They have all been so good to me. How can I leave them?*

I truly worried what would happen to the Zingers, but it was time. The smuggler took my hand and said "*Gyere!*" in Hungarian. (Come!) "We must go now!" A heavy rain fell as we took off, soaking us quickly to the bone. High above, the sky pressed down with dark, dense clouds. I had a hard time keeping up with this tall stranger. My wet hair dripped water onto my face and down my neck and I tried to shake it off. Within a few minutes into our walk, I could feel cold water sloshing in my boots. I was extremely uncomfortable but dared not say a word.

After a while my feet and mind became numb. I could neither

hear or see much; my legs carried me forward as an extension of his legs. I simply had to match his pace the best way I could. His hand held tightly to my little hand. Every time I fell back, he yanked me, and mumbled something to himself. He scared me, so I pushed myself as hard as I could, not wanting to make him angry. I had no idea where we were, or where we were going. But Kassa was already long behind us.

The rain stopped. We rested near a farmhouse and ate some food from his pack. A horse-drawn wagon filled with hay pulled up out of nowhere. The smuggler told me I was going to be hidden within the pile of hay for about an hour until we crossed the border into Slovakia. The very idea terrified me, but I had no choice.

A peasant smuggler got off the wagon, dug a hole into the center of the hay mound, and told me to climb in and lay on my stomach. I followed his directions and settled in. I pushed the hay away from the front of my face so I could breathe and lay flat on the hard, wooden floor of the wagon with some loose hay under me to buffer the bumps in the road. I could feel the weight of the thick hay mound on my back. The peasant sealed the hole but left a small opening for me to get air and some light. Suddenly, I panicked. *What if they find me? What if I suffocate? What if I have to pee?* I had never felt so helpless or vulnerable in my life.

Within a short time, I became very hot and began to cry. Once again, I felt trapped. I turned to God and recited the *Shemah Yisrael. Hear O' Israel, Lord of the Universe... please help me! I want to live!* I sobbed quietly.

Thinking of being with my Anyu and Apu again calmed me down. I began to doze off due to the rocking motion of the wagon, a gentle lull. I was awakened by a loud "Whoa, whoa!"of the coachman. The wagon stopped with a jolt. After a short silence, I picked up a conversation taking place nearby. Several men were speaking to each other. First, I could not hear them very well, but then I detected German words coming closer and closer. A feeling like terror gripped me. I felt dizzy and could hardly breathe. Could it be the border security patrol helping the Slovaks? Were they going to unload the hay and find a little Jewish boy being smuggled across the border? *Please God, don't let them find me!*

I expected the hay to be removed from the wagon, but instead, I could hear and feel something poking into the hay above my head, behind me, and in front of me. A pitchfork possibly, or a bayonet at the end of a Nazi rifle? I was petrified. I froze. I pretended I didn't even exist. Was I imagining all of this or was it really happening? Finally, the voices and the rough German chatter, stopped. I heard the sound of boots walking away. Then I heard a loud *"Dio! Dio!"* The crack of a whip and the wagon wheels began to turn again. I took a deep breath at last.

Thank you my dear God, Pán Božko, *I love you.* I tried to relax as the hay wagon kept rolling. I moved my legs, I moved my arms. I could feel my body, hear myself breathing. I definitely needed to piss. *I better hold it in until I get out of this hole.* Fear turned to anticipation. *Just a little longer,* I consoled myself, *and we will be in Prešov.*

CHAPTER 20

Prešov, A Homecoming
April 1944

After what seemed a very long time, finally, I heard the words "Whoa, whoa!" again, the peasant smuggler's command for the horses to stop. Someone removed the hay and told me to come out. It was my smuggler. This time I was happy to see his ugly face staring at me up close. I no longer feared him. I took a deep breath and inhaled some much-needed fresh air as he helped me down from the wagon. He rushed me away toward a small train station. There, he pushed me up the steps of a train carriage and told me to sit down in a compartment with a wooden bench. As soon as I did, he hung his heavy, long, black coat over me. It had a horrible stench. *What now?*

"Pretend you are asleep," he whispered as the train began to move. I was completely hidden from the passengers. There, under the dark cloak of the coat, I imagined the joyful reunion I hoped was ahead, looking forward to Anyu's delicious cooking that I loved so much, and a hot bath and my very own bed again. But what if my parents weren't even there when I arrived? We had been forced to move once. What if it had happened again while I was gone and they didn't even live at that apartment anymore? In a second, my hopes and dreams of being home were replaced by anxiety and dread and I began to perspire. I shifted slightly under the coat, leaning against the side of the train.

Before long, I heard the conductor demanding to see our tickets. I hoped he would not lift the coat. Beads of sweat ran down my face. A moment later, I felt the coat moving and heard my smuggler say, "Please don't, sir! You will wake up my son. He is sick. Here is his ticket."

Another moment of tension passed. I relaxed and closed my eyes, listening to the monotonous sounds of the wheels "*patam, patam, patam*". Within minutes, I dozed off.

I woke up to the loud voice of the conductor announcing the next stop, "Prešov! Do not forget to remove your valises on the way out." My heart started beating faster. I was so excited to get back to my parents. My emotions on edge, I felt a mixture of happiness, fatigue, fear and hope. *Where would I go if they weren't at home when I get there? What would I do?* Confusion set in. Negative thoughts tumbled through my mind. The train stopped. I wanted to get off but couldn't until he removed the coat. He was waiting for our compartment to empty out. Once more, he spoke to me in a whisper, "You get out here and start walking. I'll be behind you for a while. Don't look back. Go straight home. Good luck. Bye."

Off came the smelly coat and I darted out of the train. From the train station into the city, I pretended to belong to the stream of adults walking in the same direction. It was a Sunday morning and not too many people walked about. They were either in church or sleeping in, the streets mostly empty. Within a few minutes of entering the main street, the train crowd dispersed in different directions.

I found myself walking on my own. Suddenly, I was interrupted by a male voice calling from nearly a block away, "Hey young man, what are you doing out so early all alone? Are you lost?"

I turned my head in the direction of the sound and saw two policemen standing on the corner. Startled, I pretended not to hear them. Then I rounded a corner abruptly. As soon as they were out of sight, I took off as fast as I could run, sped through a gate, and exited on a side street. I kept running, gasping for breath, until I arrived at the big gate surrounding the apartment building and my parent's shared, cramped, back-alley living quarters. What bad luck! The gate was locked. I looked back behind me. No one on the street anywhere. I bent down, picked up a small rock, and tossed it at one of the two windows in the maid's unit where they lived. No response. A chill ran down my spine. Try again. This time I looked for a larger stone. I threw it at the window, and to my relief, soon saw my Anyu's face looking out at me, a big smile on her face. Then I heard her shout, "Frici! Hurry up! Open the gate, Osika is here!"

A moment later, I found myself inside being hugged and kissed, my face wet from my parents' tears and my own, streams of joy running down my neck onto my shirt. All of us were overwhelmed with happiness, thrilled to be together once more. Anyu helped me take off my dirty, sweaty clothes, plus my shoes and socks, and then turned on the warm water. Within a couple of minutes, I was in the tub taking a bath, so happy to be at home, but so very, very tired. Next, my Apu brought me a warm drink. Hot food awaited on the table. They both encouraged me to eat.

"Osika, have a piece of this, a little bit of that. How about your favorite cheese? A piece of *dioš kalacs* (nut strudel) or maybe *kakaos* (chocolate babka)? Do you want more coffee?" (Yes, I drank coffee as a child.)

"What I really want," I answered, "is to go to bed." I lay down on clean sheets and fell fast asleep.

"Osika, Osika! Wake up. Are you feeling alright? You have been sleeping for ten hours. It's not good to sleep that long. You must be hungry."

I opened my eyes. Was this a dream? Was I really home? My vision cleared and I saw both my parents bending over me with big, happy smiles. They sat down on the bed and again, we embraced each other, this time without tears, only with pure gratitude. For the next hour I told them all about my trip back home and my life during the past year with the Zinger family.

To my surprise, my Štaub grandparents, my Uncle Teodor, and my Aunt Ružena with her little boy Turko were all living with my parents in the same space. They had been hiding together the whole time I was living in Kassa. Thus far they had been able to avoid the Hlinka Guardists with the help of dear Doctor Šolc who was still the chief district judge for the county.

"The situation here is getting desperate," explained Anyu. "Most of our friends have been picked up and deported for hard labor and resettlement." Actually, this meant sent to the camps. Somehow I knew the labor camps were the equivalent of death. I worried I would not see my friends again.

Omama and Opapa were going to be leaving us soon. They wanted to go to a senior home in the city of *Nové Mesto nad Váhom* in western Slovakia, having heard that our government was going to protect them and other seniors from deportation. They were in great danger of being picked up here in Prešov. We wished them the best.

My parents still had the sacred white card which protected them and me from deportation and "resettlement" to Germany, but there were no guarantees anymore. The laws changed from one day to the next. At this point in our lives, no Jews were safe.

Slovak Hlinka Guard
© CTK – Photo 2022

Slovak anti-Jewish propaganda posters.
Images: public domain

CHAPTER 21

The Last Seder with My Štaub Grandparents

I returned from Kassa in time for the holiday of Pesach (or Passover). I was happy to be back home with my parents even though I left behind a more relaxed family atmosphere at the Zinger household. I missed my cousins Judit and Rŏzsi. The adults here were tense and worried. Conversations continued to take place at a very low level, almost in a whisper. We constantly listened for footsteps outside in the courtyard.

I had been helping with household chores since we were all completely housebound. They kept me busy. No one went anywhere. For grocery shopping or any other services outside of our place, we depended on my grandparents' former housekeeper, the same one who now occupied their former luxurious apartment and seemed to be enjoying it. Of course, she was more than happy to trade her back-street, humble dwelling with their beautifully furnished and decorated home. Having worked for them over twenty years, she was, thankfully, still very loyal to them and, we all hoped, trustworthy. Further, it was agreed that if the Hlinka Guardists came around looking for my grandparents, she would tell them that they left a while ago, leaving no forwarding address, and that is why she took over their apartment. Most important, she was our best link to the outside world and risked her own safety by her ongoing services to our family. Turning her back on us could have resulted in dire consequences, especially to my Aunt Ružena, her baby Turko, and my Uncle Tidi whose residency status in Prešov was illegal. If the authorities had been tipped off, we would have all been deported.

Our Passover Seder (or service) that spring was a solemn tribute to the ancient biblical events in Egypt. Apu and Grandpa Štaub were in charge of conducting the order of the centuries-old prayers but without chanting or singing. Discussion was kept at a minimum. All the windows had coverings to keep any light from shining into the courtyard. As we sat in hiding, secretly celebrating the Jewish holiday of *Pesach* (Passover), we retold the timeless story of the Jew's exodus out of ancient Egypt, themselves enslaved and worked to death by a tyrannical Pharaoh.

My participation in the Seder was limited to asking "The Four Questions", an important part of the service in the Seder text, and having a sip of wine when it was time to drink. Our meal was temporarily interrupted by Grandma Štaub choking on a stray fish bone while eating a piece of carp. Everyone came to her rescue with different suggestions as to how to remove it. Poor Omama wasn't sure who to listen to. Her coughing and choking scared all of us. We hoped she couldn't be heard from the outside. I kept hoping she wouldn't die. She drank lots of water. She ate matza. She leaned forward. She even stuck her fingers into her throat trying to reach the bone and pull it out. Finally, she calmed down. The bone seemed to pass.

The Seder service continued. But suddenly we heard footsteps near the door to the courtyard. Anyu said "*Csit csak!*" (shhh shhh) and everyone froze. No one said a word. Someone quickly turned off the lights. Total blackout. Then, a knock on the door. We did not answer. Then a second knock, much stronger. We all stopped breathing. Still one more—a harsh rapping against the wooden door. It sounded fierce and hostile. Seconds ticked by. The grownups glanced around the table with cold, fearful eyes. Then silence. The intruder appeared to be leaving. Several more minutes passed. I saw beads of sweat on my father's forehead and I had a knot in my stomach that actually hurt. Anyu exhaled slowly. Grandmother Štaub sighed and muttered a prayer in Hebrew. Then the lights came back on and the Seder continued.

Before I left for Kassa, I used to run into the bedroom and hide under my parents' bed every time we heard a loud knock on the entry door. It was a precautionary measure to protect me in the event of an unexpected visit by Hlinka Guardists bent on taking us in, in spite of our privileged status, clearly disobeying their superior's orders. That sort of behavior was not uncommon. My parents assured me that if I hid, they would always find someone to come back and fetch me if they could not get to me themselves. Then we would be reunited. I could not imagine such a thing and hoped it would never, ever come to pass.

Anyu told me that while I was in Kassa, she and Apu opened our home to Polish Jews who were illegally smuggled into Prešov and in need of temporary sanctuary, an extremely risky undertaking. She did this because the roundups had slowed for several months and she felt emboldened to do so. But if caught, she and Apu would have lost whatever protection they had. She told me that they had several close calls. If it weren't for her ability to dissuade the Guardists from searching the apartment, my parents, along with the Polish illegals, would have all been deported to a concentration camp.

Not long after Passover, I kissed my father's parents, Oma and Opa, goodbye as they left for the senior home in the remote mountain town of *Nové Mesto nad Váhom*. I hoped they would be safe there. I also said goodbye to Aunt Ružena, Turko and Uncle Teodor who all decided to go back to Bratislava, the capital of Slovakia. Lacking stereotypical East European Jewish features, blue-eyed Ružena passed for a Christian and found a job as a nanny and housekeeper with a pleasant family there. Her brother, Teodor, on the other hand, lived somewhere else in the city, but they were able to see each other occasionally. Our sad farewells left us all apprehensive, not sure if we would ever see one another again.

I knew it was just a matter of time before it would be our turn to leave Prešov, too. I was told that we now had in our possession fake baptismal birth certificates purchased from counterfeiters while I was gone. These were our only real protection and very vital ones at that.

CHAPTER 22

A New Identity
June 1944

Following a relatively quiet couple of months, searches for remaining Jews began to intensify everywhere. Almost every week someone in hiding had been found and immediately arrested. No matter their age or profession or state of health, they were picked up and taken away, possibly never to be seen again.

We realize our falsified papers were no longer of use in Prešov. Too many people knew my parents. It wouldn't take much longer before a non-Jew who was an antisemite would recognize one of us and turn us in. Even the powerful white card would not help. Therefore, one beautiful June morning, we packed our personal belongings into suitcases and rucksacks, left the keys to the front door under a mat, and piled into the back seat of a waiting taxicab. The driver was immediately inquisitive, asking questions. He wanted to know where we were going and why, and how long we were going to stay.

Anyu politely told him we were headed for a holiday to Liptovský Svätý Mikuláš, a city near the Tatra mountains that was west of Prešov and about a four hour drive away. We would pay him well for the trip. The taxi driver stopped asking questions after that.

Looking out the taxi window, I was fascinated by the sights: the trees, the green pastures, farms with flocks of sheep, cows and horses. The road trip felt similar to a train ride but without the constant clickety-clack of the wheels on the tracks. The highway was not busy. Once in a while a truck or a car came from the opposite direction. I saw many horse-drawn carriages as we drove through small towns and villages.

Anyu and Apu were unusually quiet. They must have been apprehensive and nervous, just like me. Before we left Prešov, I was told not to ask any questions in the taxi-cab. Even though the driver seemed trustworthy since he was a local resident of Prešov, we needed to be cautious and close-mouthed about our plans. Like Apu said, "These days we cannot trust anyone."

A few kilometers before Poprad, a mountain resort town not far from Mikuláš, the traffic on the westbound lane came to a halt. "What seems to be the problem?" asked Apu of the driver.

"I have no idea," he replied. "Perhaps a flock of sheep is crossing, or some cows."

The longer we waited, the paler my mother's face became. She whispered to Apu in Hungarian: *"Talán keresnek zsidókat?"* (Maybe the authorities are searching for Jews?)

I was straining to see what I could find out on my side. No traffic could be seen coming toward us in the eastbound lane. A curious passenger got out from the car ahead of us to see what the problem might be. Then another. Now there were many cars stopped behind us and people standing on the road. We felt trapped and definitely in danger of being discovered.

Without warning, a pair of light military vehicles zoomed by, followed by open trucks with soldiers in full battle gear seated on each side. Our driver announced in Slovak, "*Nemecké vojáci!*" (German soldiers!)

We froze. I could feel my heart nearly jumping out of my chest. Next, I saw a German officer walking alongside the stalled traffic directing the military convoy of cars, jeeps, ammunition trucks, tanks and supply carriers which flowed eastward like a mighty river. Another officer, followed by several more, walked by our taxi, busy with his assignment. Yet another approached wearing a different kind of hat in a handsome uniform with many decorative, colored medals on his chest. He stopped and chatted with the occupants of the car in front of ours.

Anyu whispered in my ear, "Osika, smile at him as he walks by our car." As he slowly walked toward us, I got scared, but instinctively rolled down the window, stuck my right arm out, and shouted the words "*Heil Hitler!*" in my high-pitched voice.

He approached, bent down, smiled at me, and peered into the taxi's back window, leaning in. He scanned our faces with a blank expression. "Heil Hitler!" he barked back in return and kept on walking. I turned around and saw my parents' paralyzed but smiling faces. Anyu said to me softly in Hungarian, "*Megollek!*" (I will kill you.)

At that moment, our car started moving forward slowly. The driver gunned his motor. I was totally fascinated by the cavalcade of stalled war machinery before our eyes. It appeared to me to be

a magical display of half-tracks, (open trucks with seating for soldiers), tanks of various sizes, cannons (from short ones to very long
ones), and other specialized vehicles, most of which I had never seen
before. As we finally passed the long military convoy, the tension
subsided, and we were once again able to relax.

Turning my head towards my parents, I caught a glimpse of the
beautiful, rugged peaks of the Tatra Mountains to the right of us,
rising high into the sky. I remembered learning about the Tatra in
school. They were the highest range in the Carpathian Mountains
forming a border between Poland and Czechoslovakia, cresting at
almost 9000 feet and running 35 miles in length. Slovaks liked them
for hunting and skiing. The word *tatra* in Slovak meant barren or
stony, and to me, these fierce-looking mountains were every bit of
that. I heard they were nice for hiking in summer, but treacherous
in winter, plus home to wolves and many other dangerous, wild animals.

We must be getting close to Poprad, I deducted, staring at the
mountains through the taxi window. Transportation to various summer and winter resorts departed from this attractive hub. Unexpect-
edly, Anyu caught the attention of the driver and informed him of
a sudden change in plans. She was feeling pain in her stomach and
asked him, please, to find the nearest hospital in the town of Poprad.

I was dumbfounded. I looked at her questioningly, my eyes
meeting hers. She leaned over to my father and whispered into his
ear, then turned to me and quietly explained that she had been uncomfortable for much of the journey. It should not be for long, she
reassured me. She just wanted a doctor to give her a checkup. Her
facial expression however, told me that this was a ploy. I didn't know
why she was enacting this charade, but I proceeded to calm down,

lean back and smile at her. She smiled back.

Shortly thereafter, the taxi parked in front of the Poprad hospital. Apu assisted Anyu in getting out of the car. He told the driver to wait while we escorted my mother into the hospital, and within minutes she was admitted. We were told by a nun, referred to as "Sister", that "Pani (Mrs.) Šťambova (my mother's new name on her falsified baptismal certificate) will have to stay overnight for various checkups and tests." Then she added, "Visiting hours are from six to eight in the evening. You are welcome to come back and visit her during those hours."

My father and I returned to the taxi. "Can you take us to the closest hotel, please?" requested Apu. Within minutes we checked into a small but clean hotel under our new names of Fredrich Šťamba and Ondrej Šťámba, religious affiliation—Catholic. A perfect cover. Before we entered the hotel, Apu paid the car fare and bid goodbye to the taxi. As we entered our room, a weird feeling came over me. Apu and I looked at each other and we both began to cry. *What were we doing? Was Anyu going to be safe there?* He hugged and consoled me. *"Neboj sa Osika,"* he said in Slovak. (Don't be afraid Osika. Everything will be okay.)

CHAPTER 23

Leaving Poprad

Both of us were exhausted and fell onto the bed to catch some sleep. My father woke me saying, "Let's get some food before we go back to the hospital." We found a restaurant nearby, ate together quietly and then walked to the hospital. The distance was only about half a mile, the mountain air quite refreshing.

We learned at the registrar's desk that Anyu's room was on the second floor. It was almost seven o'clock. We had an hour to visit. A nurse was attending to her as we walked in and Anyu was moaning as if in pain. We waited until the nurse was done and then told us that we may go in. We sat down and Anyu explained what the preliminary findings of the attending physician indicated. It turned out, not much. They wouldn't know more until after the blood and other tests were concluded. Then Anyu told us in a hushed whisper that her sudden decision to check into the hospital was really more a matter of buying some time than anything else. She was not sick.

"We have to figure out our next course of action, Frici," she said.

"We must be careful not to run into someone from Prešov. That would be the end. Meanwhile, you'll both be safer staying in the hotel."

Our conversation seemed strained. There was not much we could talk about openly. We were worried that someone might be listening outside the door. Anyu asked us to bring her some food the next day. She said the hospital food was tasteless. Of course, she couldn't eat the hospital food. It was treif, not kosher. The hour went fast. My mood improved once I understood what was going on. The next day we supplied Anyu with dairy foods purchased at a nearby grocery.

On the third day, we walked in and noticed that she was pale, with a concerned look on her face. "Why are you so pale, *mamička?* (mommy)?" I asked.

"*Mi van veled?*" echoed Apu in Hungarian. (Did the doctor find something wrong?) Anyu asked me to check the hallway. I went out. No one was there. As I re-entered her room, Apu was sitting on her bed listening intently as Anyu spoke in a bare whisper. I asked, "What's the matter?"

"I'll tell you after we leave," he replied. Glancing at the door, Anyu added, "Not to worry. Apu will tell you everything."

Agitated, I was growing impatient. I was entitled to know what was happening. Nudging his arm, I said, "Let's go already, I'm tired." He relented, we both kissed Anyu good night, and left. In the hallway Apu said, "Let's find the back staircase and exit through the back door." Once we were out of the building, he checked to see if the door opened from the outside. It did. "Good," he reassured himself. A few steps away from the hospital I asked him, "Apu, please tell me what *is* going on?"

He explained that the head nurse, the nun, had been asking Anyu too many questions. She might be suspecting something. Anyu was becoming restless and fearful. Medically, the doctor had not found anything wrong with her stomach. He was very nice and friendly, but Anyu thought that the nun might have been an antisemite, liable to alert the authorities. She felt her safety was jeopardized.

"Osika, we'll have to get up very early in the morning, enter through the back door, and smuggle her out of her room," said Apu.

What? Smuggle my mother out? Like pirates? I was shocked. I reminded Apu that whatever we did, he better be sure a taxi was waiting for us when we snuck out of the hospital. We had to be able to head out of town right away before the nurse discovered an empty bed and no sign of "Mrs. Irena Šťambova."

Before retiring for the night, Apu checked us out of the hotel. We packed and readied our suitcases, placed a summer dress into a paper bag for Anyu, and laid down. I was too nervous to sleep. The whole thing sounded too exciting to me.

The alarm clock woke me up. Apu rushed around the room placing suitcases and other bags by the door. I wondered if he even slept during the night. While I got dressed and washed, a local taxi pulled up as scheduled. Apu and the driver loaded the baggage into the trunk. It was still dark. We arrived at the hospital, got out and headed to the back door. Not a sound anywhere. Apu and I mounted the steps, quietly carrying the bag with Anyu's dress. We snuck into her room. She was wide awake, anticipating our arrival, and dressed quickly. Within minutes we were on our way down the stairs and out of the hospital to the waiting taxi.

Apu said to the driver, "Take us to Mikuláš, please." Within minutes, the car was on the highway heading west. Dawn broke to a clear morning sky. On our right, the deep blue Tatra Mountains reflected the bright sunlight, beckoning a fine day. All around us nature was waking up, filling our hearts with joy and hope. With Anyu in the middle, Apu and I sat next to her like a pair of bookends, supporting her with our love. Our little family was back together again, pushing forward to the next chapter of survival.

CHAPTER 24

Under Cover in Mikuláš

W e drove into Mikuláš, a small mountain town located above the Vah River Valley by mid-morning. Anyu asked the driver to slow down since she wanted to read any "FOR RENT" signs on the houses. Looking all around, Apu noted, "This town seems similar in size to Prešov. I like that. And both towns are filled with tourists year-round because of their closeness to the mountains, which means lots of strangers. I like that even more. Best of all, we don't know a soul here, and that's good for us."

I was glad. I liked Mikuláš right away. It looked pretty and somehow, felt safe.

The taxi drove around town searching for a rental sign. Nothing appeared for some time. Then the driver stopped abruptly in front of a house with a "FOR RENT" sign in a second floor window. My parents got out, telling me to wait in the car. The driver meanwhile started asking questions about my school and what kinds of books I liked to read, but I was not too friendly. I was being cautious, giving him half-answers and pretending not to hear. He must have thought I was rude, so he stopped talking.

Luckily, Apu returned within a few minutes. He told the driver we were staying and to please help remove our luggage from the trunk. He motioned to me saying, "Osika, help me carry our things upstairs."

I was more than happy to help. I jumped out of the car and grabbed a couple of small bags. My mother came out of the building to assist. In Hungarian, she told Apu to give the driver a generous tip. Curious to see our new place, I ran up the steps, entered an open door where I was greeted by an elderly man with grayish hair who I quickly learned was a retired minister — and the owner of the apartment. He led me to the room my parents had just rented. I dumped the bags and ran straight to the window. *This is great!* I thought to myself. *We are high up on the second floor and the view overlooks the town, facing the main street.* As the taxi pulled away, I noticed more of our bags left on the sidewalk so I went back downstairs and helped carry them in.

Once settled, I wanted to know which was my bed. Anyu pointed to the couch. Of course, I had to try it out, so I lay down with a bang! She told me in an angry voice that I must be quiet and courteous to the elderly couple who were our landlords, and to their furniture and not draw attention to myself.

"Make sure you don't ever slip up about who we really are," reminded Apu. "They did not want any children here, but I told him what a wonderful boy you are and promised you wouldn't cause any trouble."

"Don't worry," I replied. "*Budem dobry.*" (I'll be good.)

We soon celebrated our first Friday night in Mikuláš. Anyu prepared a very simple meal for dinner, not the nicer Sabbath menu we had come to expect. She made plain, boiled chicken with mashed potatoes and cooked vegetables. Before we sat down, and in almost secrecy, she quietly lit two candles like she always did and recited the usual Sabbath blessing in Hebrew in a soft and melodious voice. Then Apu proceeded with the *kiddush*, the blessing over the wine, whispering the prayer so we could barely hear him. He gave me a sip from his *kiddush* cup. It did not taste like wine, rather, like some sort of juice. As I drank, I noticed tears in Apu's eyes. I looked away and pretended not to see them. Next, Anyu blew out the candles. (According to tradition, Sabbath candles must burn out on their own). We needed to conserve them. Then she went to the kitchen to get the food. She had to be very careful because she shared the kitchen with the minister's wife. After all, they had no idea we were Jewish. This added much tension to our daily life and to every meal.

Following the wine, we each made a silent blessing over the bread unlike the traditional blessing typically sung out loud. In a strange, tense atmosphere, we proceeded to eat without any conversation. That night became the rehearsal for many future, secret Shabbat and holiday celebrations. Anyu told me during dinner that we must maintain our religious traditions faithfully if we wanted God to help us survive these terribly dangerous times.

"Osika, make sure you say your prayers every day," my mother reminded.

I tried. We couldn't go to a synagogue under the circumstances, so we prayed at home. I had to be careful when I went outside and make very sure that my *tzitzit* didn't hang out of my shorts. These are the fringes or tassels worn on traditional garments by Jewish males as commanded in the Bible. Some are shorter than others for kids. All Orthodox Jewish boys wore them.

Every morning, my father put on his *tallis*, his prayer shawl, phylacteries and tefillin, a small black leather box worn on the forehead containing Hebrew texts on parchment with black straps for the forearms, a reminder to keep the law. These were and still are worn by observant adult Jews during morning prayers.

Apu prayed for a few minutes before he ate breakfast. Watching him all wrapped up in his long prayer shawl, bowing and bending his upper torso repeatedly as he prayed, made me feel secure, protected by the holy presence of *Pán Božko*, also known as *Adonai* in Hebrew. Whatever we called him, I knew God was always with us.

CHAPTER 25

Partisans Attack!

Within a short time, Apu was very lucky to find work in a local box factory. He left early every morning to get there by eight o'clock. With my father having a job and keeping a roof over our heads, I felt very fortunate to be in Mikuláš.

From time-to-time, Allied bombers, either from Great Britain, the Soviet Union or America, would fly over the city in large formations in their effort to push back the Germans. I would get so excited that when the sirens blared, I put on my best clothes, went down to the street, and waved my hands at the planes. Although we didn't yet see or hear the war raging, they were a clear reminder that a war was happening around us.

Anyu and I did not go out very much. She was always worried that someone from Prešov, especially a Fascist visiting Mikuláš, might recognize her and turn us in to the authorities. For some reason, she always took me with her grocery shopping or wherever else she went, even more than before when we lived in Prešov. Many times, I preferred to stay home and read my books or draw pictures, but she insisted I go with her.

On Sundays, I was allowed to play with local children on the sidewalk in front of our building. A few were my age. We talked and played games like hopscotch or raced from one end of the block to the other. There was hardly any traffic on our street other than pedestrians on the sidewalk. One of us would often cross the street and we would kick a ball back and forth until we got interrupted by an occasional passing car or horse-drawn carriage.

Sunday was my day to be a kid. I really enjoyed being with others my age, but sometimes, I wished I had a brother. I could have had more fun. Being an only child, spending most of the time with my parents and other adults, often made me sad. Everyone was so very serious. They expected me to be like them. I didn't dare crack a joke or act funny. It was hard to be myself.

One Saturday midmorning, I was reciting some of the *shacharit* or morning blessings that Apu taught me the year before when I was distracted by loud noises outside the open window. My curiosity interrupted my devotional task. I laid down my siddur and walked to the window. Carriage after carriage drawn by galloping horses, furiously whipped by their drivers, filled the streets. Some were empty, others packed with entire families or various household items. Here and there a truck rolled by passing the carriages, sounding their horns. I also detected popping sounds coming from the direction of the city center. Boom! Pop, pop, pop!

"Anyu, Anyu!" I called out. "Something strange is going on down below. Come see."

"I am busy now, Osika."

I looked back and saw that she was sitting in the rocking chair praying, so I left her alone. Meanwhile, the sidewalk across the street was filling with pedestrians walking fast in the same direction as the traffic, away from the center of town. Some men were actually running barefoot, some half-naked, carrying their clothes in their hands. I focused my eyes on a tall runner and realized he was a soldier. A German soldier like the ones I had seen along the highway from the taxicab!

Anyu joined me at the window and saw all the commotion down below. "*Istenem!*" (Oh my God!) she said in Hungarian. German soldiers running away from the city. There must be a conflict. I hope Apu is alright."

My heart pounded with joy. A miracle! German soldiers leaving the city, but barefooted? About an hour later, Apu came home, extremely excited. "You won't believe what is happening!"

"What's going on? Tell us!" We all gathered around the table. Anyu asked further, "*Mi történt?*" (What happened?)

Apu explained, "I was working, loading the folding machine to help fulfill an order of 2000 boxes to be delivered next week. All of a sudden, we heard loud explosions and automatic rifle shots coming from the direction of the central plaza. We all stopped. The racket went on for about half an hour. Our boss told us to leave everything and come into the building so no one would get hurt from stray bullets. We stayed out of sight for a long time. When it all quieted down, one of our employees came back from an errand, clearly upset. He had been caught in the firefight and was nearly struck by a bullet when the violence broke out."

"Apu, who was shooting?" I wanted to know everything.

Apu continued. "I heard that it started when three taxicabs drove to the plaza and stopped opposite the German headquarters. Seven Slovak partisans jumped out of the cars, dispersed, and took positions surrounding the building. They were all heavily armed, carrying automatic weapons and grenades. The plaza quickly emptied with people running in all directions and the attack began. The partisans demanded that the entire German garrison of about 200 soldiers surrender. The German soldiers began to shoot from the second-story windows. Within minutes of the first explosions, groups of Slovak soldiers from nearby camps pulled up in trucks and joined the partisans in the uprising. The Germans were surprised and overwhelmed. Many were shot. Total chaos erupted. As the partisans and Slovak renegade soldiers gained the upper hand, many startled Germans jumped out of the second floor windows in the back of the building and simply began to run to save themselves from being killed. After about an hour, those trapped inside surrendered."

"Apu, we saw them running barefoot!" I added. "Many of them were half-naked, on our street! Some of our neighbors standing on the sidewalk under our window applauded, laughing and jeering. I heard somebody yelling, 'Hold on to your pants!' It was really scary but at the same time, funny, too."

"*Mi lesz most?*" asked Anyu in Hungarian, her eyes wide with worry. (What will happen now?)

"We'll have to wait and see," answered Apu, but he looked concerned too.

Our landlords came to our room when they heard that Apu

knew what had taken place at the city center. Together we listened to Apu's description of the events that shook up the city of Mikuláš all over again.

Soon the street below was abandoned. A hopeful atmosphere surrounded us. *Will the German army retaliate? Will we suffer for this attack?* Apu said we can only hope for the best.

Good news spreads fast. The following day several units of the Slovak infantry stationed in the vicinity under the command of a young colonel secured the city, declaring it a "Free Zone." The Fascist leadership escaped alongside their German Nazi protectors. Those who stayed behind were arrested and charged with treason. The threat was gone, overnight! Life in this city blossomed without the yoke of the German army. We cherished our sudden freedom.

Heroic Slovak Partisans – 1944
Photo: public domain

CHAPTER 26

News from the Outside
1944

$\mathbf{A}$nyu and I took long walks exploring the quaint neighborhoods, shops and parks of Mikuláš. We even surprised Apu at his place of work one day. At first he wasn't sure it was a smart idea but in a short time, his co-workers and his boss welcomed us in a friendly manner. We continued to maintain our non-Jewish identity, pretending we were Christians. One day, as we were traversing the central plaza, Anyu recognized a Jewish woman who occasionally shopped in my parents' store in Prešov. It stopped her in her tracks. She was one of us, a Jew in hiding like ourselves.

Through her acquaintance we befriended other Jews who were also fugitives from the Slovak governments' anti-Jewish laws who were also hiding in Mikuláš under aliases, posing as Christians. Following the uprising and our newfound sense of freedom, we were encouraged and inspired by our ability to attend religious services held in the recently reactivated synagogue. Attendance was minimal. Even though we all expected that the Nazi army would most likely return and recapture the city at some point, every moment of freedom was precious. My parents now met their new Jewish friends, played cards with them, and exchanged all sorts of information openly and without fear.

The biggest news circulating in Jewish circles at that time had to do with the miraculous escape of a small group of Jews from the Auschwitz concentration camp. Somehow, two of them ended up behind bars in the police jail in Mikuláš. No one knew exactly how they came to be here. The name of one of the prisoners happened to be Arnošt Rozin.

Anyu, surprised and excited, said, "*Jaj* (Oh!), I have a second cousin by that name. I wonder if this could be him?" She inquired if anyone among her card playing partners had connections to the police. Sure enough, she got the name of the officer in charge of the jail and found out that Mr. Rozin was in solitary confinement and could not have visitors. But that didn't stop my dear mother. She was determined to see if it was him and maybe, even get him out of jail.

The next morning, after breakfast, Anyu told me to put on my best clothes and shoes because I was going with her to the police station jail to see her cousin. But she would be careful to still hide her identity. I was scared. I had a flashback to the police station in Kassa. "What if they decide to lock us up? Why don't you take Apu instead?"

"Apu is working, you know that. He cannot come. Did I ever let you down, Osika?" my mother replied. " Don't worry."

I put my fears aside and chugged along with my brave Anyu. After a half hour walk, we entered the police station and she inquired about the police officer whose name she was given. The receptionist answered abruptly, "*Dnes tu nie je.*" (He is not here today.)

"But I spoke with him yesterday and he told me to come in today, that he would let me visit my old school friend Arnošt Rozin whom I have not seen since I was a little girl." My mother was clever not to identify herself as a Jew. At that point the jailer called in a policeman. "Sit down," he ordered us.

We sat and waited quietly for a long time. I grew bored and restless. I whispered to Anyu, "Let's go home and come back tomorrow." She scowled at me, shaking her head. After a long while, the door opened and a police officer entered. Anyu straightened up, put on a big smile, and repeated the same story she told the jailer.

"Madam, I don't have the authority to let you see him. It's out of my jurisdiction. The captain will be back from Bratislava tomorrow."

Anyu interrupted, turned on her charm, and told him we had to catch a train the next day, early in the morning. "Surely you could just give me five minutes to say hello to him, dear officer." She put her hand on his arm and looked straight into his face. He smiled at her and said meekly, "*Poďte zo mnou.*" (Come with me.)

Anyu turned around, gave me her unusual look of assurance and said, "*Poď Osika, poď.*" (Come.) I followed them through a hallway, then down a few steps to the jail. We stopped in front of a barred cell.

"*Pán Rozin, niekto vás chce vidieť!*" (Somebody wants to see you.)

From the shadows, a lean person in striped prisoner's garb appeared behind the bars and peered out, staring at Anyu.

"Ernö?" she asked, calling him by his name in Hungarian.

"*Igen?*" he answered. (Yes?)

"*Grünfeld, Irén,*" said Anyu, reminding him of their birthplace. "*Sobránce.*" Remember?"

"Irénke!" he exclaimed and reached for her through the bars. Tears spilled from their eyes as they grasped each other's' hands. At that point, the jailer said, "*Päť minuty.*" (five minutes) and left. Five minutes then turned to half an hour at least.

Ernö told Anyu about his ordeal, the escape with the other prisoners, and the many days of running, hiding, starving and stealing food and clothes from peasants when they could.

The time passed quickly. The emotional flow of words ended when the jailer came back and asked Anyu to leave. He got very angry when she ignored him, and they continued talking. But finally, she and Ernö said goodbye, hoping to see one another sometime after the war ended.

I did not hear the entire conversation because Anyu told me to go sit on a nearby bench. It was clear she didn't want me to hear all of his story. Certain aspects of what he said must have upset her quite deeply, however. I saw her cover her face with her hands sometimes, wipe away tears and shake her head in disbelief. I could see the emotion expressed on his part as he shared the horrors of Auschwitz, evidently described to her in great detail. His shoulders shook and his hands trembled, and he spoke in a great hurry, his words tumbling out, punctuated by wracking sobs.

That same evening, much of what Anyu heard from Ernö was conveyed to the close circle of new acquaintances, all Jewish friends. I was asked to go to another room, but I stayed behind the door where they couldn't see me. In hushed tones, Anyu described the systematic extermination of the prisoners, men, women and children, just as Erno had explained it to her. She spoke of the nauseous smell of the crematoriums where people were gassed to death, then burned, and the hideous smoke in the air, all day and all night. She described the misery of the thousands of innocents, starving prisoners, awaiting their fate. The terrifying cruelty he had witnessed and shared with her exceeded all the rumors that had been filtering in.

When I questioned her later about what I "accidentally" overheard, she replied, "Osika, I told you. You don't need to know everything." So I dropped it. Again, I knew she was only trying to protect
me.

Truly, I was too young to hear about such horrible things and
wished afterward that I had not, and could shut it all out. But it was
too late. I knew in a way what was going on. It was impossible not to.
The meeting with Ernö Rozin made one thing very clear. My understanding of the world as a safe and loving place had changed forever
and the short meeting with him and my mother played a significant
role in the future plans made by my parents and the small group of
Jews in Mikuláš, all alerted and now fully informed by his miraculous escape and the undisputable, horrifying reality.

Adolf Grünfeld, Arnošť Rozin, and my father Bedrich Štaub, c. 1947

CHAPTER 27

Time to Move On

Whe news reached us that a significant buildup of German troops was taking place in our Vah Valley, new precautions had to be taken. The probability of total encirclement was growing more and more real. Mikuláš was no longer safe. My parents inquired about the feasibility of moving to a smaller town or even a village in the greater vicinity of the mountains. They gathered information on the availability of housing and the general character of the population. Would the new location welcome city folks or would the community be unfriendly?

Two villages were recommended favorably: Žiar in the east and Bobrovček in the west. Before long, the dreaded, fateful day finally arrived. An ultimatum from the commander of the Nazi military force warned the leadership of the liberated city of Mikuláš that if the partisans didn't retreat peacefully, a retaliatory offensive by the Wehrmacht, the armed forces of Nazi Germany, would destroy the city. Civilian casualties were sure to be high.

Within hours, the Slovak partisans headed out into the countryside, closer to the Tatra Mountains. The concerns among our Jewish
friends pointed to the urgency for us to leave as well. Under great
tension and anxiety, we started packing our suitcases and rucksacks,
filling them with non-perishable food and additional items we had
acquired the last couple of days. I begged my father to buy me a
small hatchet. At first my parents questioned the need and resisted. I
continued to insist until Apu agreed. He took me to a camping supply store that specialized in mountain climbing and outdoor survival equipment. I picked a double-edged, sharp hatchet with a short,
shiny, blonde wood handle. It came with a leather protective cover. I
wore it proudly tucked behind my belt, my proudest possession. Too
bad I didn't have it when I was bullied and harassed by the Christian kids after school back in Prešov. I could have scared them off or
beaten them back with my hatchet.

It was early in the morning one day in August, 1944. We were all
packed and downing a quick breakfast. The taxicab was supposed
to arrive any minute. We expressed our gratitude to our landlords
and said our goodbyes. By now we felt certain they had known we
were Jewish and accepted us. We assumed they figured it out on their
own and kept it to themselves. Apu and Anyu informed the cab driver that we did not want to be victims of the German soldiers' fury
when they recaptured Mikuláš and that was why we were going to
the countryside.

"Once things settle down in the city, we will return home," said Anyu. My parents proceeded to pump the driver for information about the various small towns and villages in the vicinity of the mountains. "What is life like in Žiar? And the people there?" Anyu asked. "And in Bobrovček?"

"Well, if you like being at the foot of the mountains, close to the forest, and like picking mushrooms and raspberries," he answered, "then you should try finding a place in Bobrovček, a nice little village. The citizens are friendly, peaceful people. Would you like me to drive you there?"

This sounded like a decent, viable option for us. Very appealing. "Let's take his advice," said Apu.

"But none of our friends ever mentioned this village, Frici," said Anyu doubtfully. "We really know nothing about it."

"The partisans have set up their headquarters in Bobrovček," added the driver. "You might also feel safer there."

"Alright, then, let's go!" replied Anyu, resolved that this was the right place.

I am sure Anyu liked the idea of having the protection of the partisans, so we were on our way to a brand new adventure. I had never lived in a mountain village. In fact, I thought to myself, this might be a lot of fun. I just hoped the peasants did not find out somehow that we were Jewish. We wouldn't stand a chance. The ride to Bobrovček didn't last too long, maybe thirty minutes.

The small village, divided in length by a narrow creek, was less than two miles long, up a hill. The main street had a long row of small, freshly painted houses on each side of the slow- moving, crystal clear water. Several simple bridges connected the two sides. The main road into Bobrovček ran along the left bank of the creek. I didn't see any villagers, only a few stray dogs. We traveled slowly, looking for any locals. Then, our driver decided to cross over a bridge to the other side. Once we did, we saw an older woman by the side of the road. She stared at our car, so we stopped. Anyu rolled down the back window and asked her in Slovak if she knew of any place for rent. She just stood there without saying a word but as the car started moving forward, she came closer and pointed to the north, further up the road.

We kept driving, looking for an empty house. Suddenly, I spotted one, got all excited, and yelled, "Here it is! Look! A little white house off to the side with a "For Rent" sign posted on the gate."

Apu got out and knocked on the door of the adjacent residence. A young peasant woman came to the door with keys in her hand, then led us through the small, but very clean, furnished house—one bedroom, a small kitchen, a metal sink for washing clothes and an antique-looking, cast iron tub. A wooden outhouse stood in the back. The rent was reasonable. We could move in that very day.

A short time later we were in our new home. Everything was very simple and rather primitive. Never mind, at least we had shelter. The landlords were happy to have us as tenants. As was customary in Slovakia, they brought over a small freshly baked loaf of bread and a basket of fruit from their fruit trees as welcome gifts. After hearing our story and the reason for moving from Mikuláš to Bobrovček, they complimented us for making a wise decision. "Not to worry, we will take good care of you."

Their two young boys, Janõš and Juray, became my new friends. They gave me a tour of the village, mostly on our side of the creek. The other side was not too friendly to boys our age, besides there were a few nasty dogs whose owners let them loose to scare us away. I did not mind small dogs. They reminded me of my little Muki that ran away from me in Prešov. Once in a while, I still thought about him and missed him. He was my best friend. Until this day, I still can't figure out why he ran away.

Here, I saw plenty of small dogs to play with. They roamed around freely as did the local ducks and roosters. My friends also showed me the house where the partisans lived. No one could walk in without an invitation. A sentry with a rifle guarded the house day and night. When we drove here in the taxi, a partisan stopped us and asked our driver and my parents all sorts of questions before he allowed us to enter the village. I hoped to befriend these brave fighters. If I were their age, I would want to be a partisan and fight the Nazis too.

I observed that much of the day these fighters stayed indoors and slept. A few days following our arrival, I learned that after dark they snuck out of the village in small groups to conduct sabotage acts against enemy targets. They ambushed military transports and blew up railroad tracks to derail trains carrying weapons and ammunitions. I was told they got their orders from a coordinated command center strategically connected to the advancing Russian army on the Polish side of the Tatra Mountains. I was in awe of them.

When Apu listened to broadcasts on our secret short-wave radio, he had a good memory for details and explained everything to me afterwards. Back in Mikuláš, when he and Anyu played cards with their new friends, deep political discussions took place between the men, while the ladies talked about cooking, trying to keep kosher under difficult circumstances, and other women's concerns. Then, as now, I always listened to my father's conversations. My Apu tried to keep me informed with the progress of the war, yet shielded me from the worst. It never failed that the local news report always said the Nazis were winning. But if we listened to the BBC, we heard what we felt was the real truth. We relied on these reports for a sense of what was really happening across Europe and the rest of the world. It seemed chaotic.

Our small house in Bobrovček.

CHAPTER 28

Peasant Life

Thankfully, our life in the village was peaceful. We kept to ourselves and no one seemed bothered by our presence. Although the
peasants were religious people, they did not impose Christian customs and practices on us. We were known as the agnostics, people
with no religion. As before, we managed to maintain our customs
secretly, behind closed doors and well-secured curtains. Once in a
while, our landlords invited us for dinner so Anyu offered to cook
and teach the wife how to prepare new dishes. That way we could
avoid having to eat their food which was not kosher and heavy on
pork and wild game.

Our village usually smelled of roasted pork on weekends. Families got together to prepare a picnic. It started with killing the pig. I
got terribly upset listening to the pig's squeals as it was repeatedly hit
on the head with big hammers, a horrible, inhumane act. Jews were
and are not allowed to eat pork, so I was not familiar with killing
pigs. But I knew we tried to butcher our animals (cows, chickens and

sheep) in a humane way, one of the main reasons behind keeping Kosher. Meanwhile, the whole neighborhood could hear the commotion and the accompanying chaos. Some pigs died hard. Then, the men drove a long skewer through the dead pig, propped it up on each end on specially made stands, and lit a large bonfire under it. Once the pig was roasted, the meal began. Anyone was invited to join in and taste the savory meat. Sometimes they roasted a lamb, which was less hectic. A lamb died much faster after they simply cut its throat. I considered all these celebrations inhumane. How could they torture these poor, defenseless animals? The village kids seemed not to be affected by any of it. This was their way of life.

What I liked best was the harvest. Our neighbors owned a piece of land where they grew wheat. Once summer came to an end the peasants rode out to harvest their fields. All the members of the family helped out. To my delight, the boys invited me to go with them. They wanted to show me, the city kid, how things were done during a harvest. I got permission from Anyu and Apu to join them. "Just be careful and don't hurt yourself" was their advice. "*Daj pozor Osika.*" (Be careful.)

I gave them a hug and a kiss and jumped on to a two-wheel flatbed with all of the family, a vehicle drawn by two big, strong oxen. We traveled on a dirt road uphill, leaving Bobrovček. I got tossed around by bumps in the road. The view of the area was beautiful, and the fields smelled fragrant, fresh and hearty. After a lengthy ride, we stopped and jumped off. We all had to carry tools into the field that we would be harvesting that day. The wheat was high, and we had to cut it down. Everyone had an assignment. I was told to watch how some of the tools were used, and then tell them when I was ready to lend a hand. Watching them cut down, sort out, and bundle the stalks reminded me of a ballet I saw once with the Zingers at the Hungarian National Theater in Kassa. The villagers' movements as they used the scythe were beautifully coordinated and precisely timed. In my head, I could hear music accompanying every stroke, every stop. I even gave it a name, "The Harvest Sonata." Before long, my turn came to jump in and become one of the dancers in this harvest ballet.

"Jánõš, teach me how to use the sickle," I said. At first, I thought it would be easy. But when I tried to use it, I had to get used to its weight and to the special wrist movements. As sharp as it was, I had to swing hard or else it did not cut down enough stalks. The first time around I wasn't much help, I was mostly practicing to get it right. The boys had a few good laughs on my account watching me fumble. I was determined to learn and be good at it, just like my friends.

At noon, the work stopped for lunch. The landlady unwrapped a white cloth that contained a large block of *slanina*, slab bacon, a couple of large onions which the locals ate like apples, and freshly baked bread. At first I wasn't sure if I should eat the bacon, wondering if maybe God would punish me for eating *chazer* (pork). Pig meat is one of the prohibited foods in the Bible.

"A piece of bread – *chleb* – will be fine," I said.

"Ondrej, try a piece of the *slanina*. It was in the smoker all night. Delicious!" Reluctantly, I relented and took a piece with a slice of onion on a chunk of bread.

"You are right. It tastes good! Thank you." (*Silently, in my head, I asked God to please not punish me. I was hungry).* I ate with great gusto. I returned home late in the afternoon, exhausted but happy. This went on for the next two weeks. I got better with the sickle and the scythe and was able to actively participate in the first harvest of my life. I learned a great deal about peasant life. The people worked hard. The men were rough, tough and demanding. The women tended the house and the garden. They raised the kids, bathed them, cut their hair, hand-washed the clothing, and made sure the meals were ready on time. The men tended to get drunk on weekends and they disciplined their kids with a belt or stick.

I was usually a quiet kid and didn't cause or get into any trouble. But one afternoon, as I was walking home, a group of boys started calling me names from the other side of the creek. I just kept walking, minding my own business. Suddenly came a barrage of rocks. A sizeable, sharp one hit me on the back of my head. It stung hard. I felt pain and got a little dizzy. I reached back and felt blood gushing down my neck and in a panic, started to cry. A villager came to me, asked where I lived, and walked home with me, calming me down. Before reaching our house, Anyu appeared. Someone alerted her to my mishap. When I told her what happened, she yelled at the kids who were laughing and calling me a coward-sissy. She threatened to cross the creek and punish them. That was the first and last time those kids bothered me. The wound healed after about two weeks and I can say that, unlike some of my worst memories from grade school, at least this time I wasn't called a dirty, stinking Jew.

As the days ticked by, I often wondered how long we could keep this pretense up and what would happen to us? The outside world was falling to pieces and we were caught in a strange play, pretending to be something we weren't. Would anyone ever help us?

CHAPTER 29

Ondrej Rides A Horse

One of our neighbors in Bobrovček owned a white horse that liked to walk in the shallow creek. The neighbor tied a rope around the horse's neck and used it like a leash while he walked on the bank alongside. Fascinated, I watched this weekly ceremony while standing in front of our rented house. One Sunday, standing close to the creek when the horse and its owner walked by, I asked him if he ever rode this horse. He looked at me with a smile and said in Slovak, "*Keď koň bol mladý.*" (I did when the horse was young. Now it is old, a retired work horse.)

"I have never been on a horse," I remarked.

"Would you like to ride him?" he asked. Before I could answer, he asked me to tell him my name.

"Ondrej Šťamba," I quickly replied. This was my made-up name printed on my falsified baptismal certificate that had been arranged for me, right along with my parents' certificates. If we were ever stopped by Fascists or Nazi collaborators, these documents would serve to prove we were non-Jews. Many people in the village already knew me by this name.

"And yes," I added. "I would like to ride," sizing up the horse. Then I got scared just thinking about sitting up so high. Sometimes horses get angry and throw off their riders. As if he were reading my mind, the owner said, "Ondrejku, my horse is very gentle. Come, I'll help you mount him. He is safe." He picked me up and told me to straddle the horse's back. The horse had nothing on him except the rope around his neck. At that moment, I was really sorry that I let the owner put me in this situation. I was scared of the horse and scared for not first asking my parent's permission. It was too late by then. I heard a smack on the horse's rear end, and it began to move forward.

"What do I do now?" I yelled as I began to tilt to the right.

"Ondrejku, grab the horse's mane. Sit up straight. Don't be afraid. I am holding on to the rope."

This was my first horseback riding lesson. With every additional step the horse took, I became less fearful and more comfortable. The owner advised, "If you want it to walk faster, just kick your heels, hard, into its belly." I followed his advice and the horse responded. Wow! I started to bounce as the horse began to pick up its feet, holding on for dear life.

"Ondrejku!" he called out again. "Hang on to the rope around his neck and don't act like you're afraid." He told me this while running alongside the creek, holding on to the rope. The horse was trotting now, and I was shaking, pulling its mane, and yelling "Whoa, whoa! Stop, stop!" to no avail. Then the owner let go of the rope.

I saw a bridge ahead. "Oh my dear God, what do I do now?" Pulling on its mane and the rope, yelling "whoa, whoa" did not help. The horse had its own mind! It stopped abruptly before the bridge, turned around, and started running the other way. I held on so hard that my hands were hurting. I finally relaxed and entrusted myself to the horse. The lesson I learned was to allow the horse to use its own head. This was a smart horse. After a few minutes, the horse stopped and the owner helped me dismount. Next time, I would not be so scared. And thus, every week, I was able to ride this gentle, wise horse, bareback. Before I left the house, Anyu always said, "*Daj pozor na seba.*"(Be careful! Take care of yourself.)

I was very proud of myself, even though I still needed help to get on and off. Someday, I promised myself, I will master that, too.

While I was having fun with the local children, my parents preferred to stay indoors. They read books, cooked meals, washed clothes, prayed and ventured out occasionally to buy groceries and necessities. A small variety store was open every day except Sundays. Much of what we needed in food we could purchase directly from the peasants. Many of them grew vegetables and fruits and raised chickens, geese, ducks, and other domestic animals, more than they could consume.

In the village, just about everyone went to church except people like us. Religious processions on Sunday mornings were led by a young man carrying a large wooden crucifix and chanting hymns, sometimes to the accompaniment of musicians. Young women wore colorful folk costumes. The air smelled of incense. On some Sunday afternoons, weather permitting, a group of peasants raced each other on their best horses.

Summer was coming to an end. The leaves were starting to fall and the nights were getting cooler. We felt very fortunate to have been protected by the partisan unit based in our village. Many surrounding villages and small towns had been overrun by para-military units of the Hlinka guards and people had been arrested. My family, perhaps more than others, appreciated and understood the significance of the partisans' presence. Anyu encouraged me to befriend them. I tried entering their headquarters but, in spite all of my gimmicks, I failed. So, I used a different strategy with my parents' consent. Two or three times a week, I would walk down to the edge of our village to visit with the sentries guarding the main road leading into Bobrovček. They were happy to have someone to talk to. For me, the main fascination was the weaponry they possessed. To touch a rifle or to hold a grenade was a real treat. I was elated just to be able to sit on the ground and have a conversation with a Slovak or Czech partisan. Over time, I learned that these young warriors were brave freedom fighters from several different countries who volunteered to fight the Nazis with unconventional methods. Most of their sabotage was conducted under the cover of darkness and in enemy territory which included Slovak Fascist government installations. These included important targets like oil and gas reserves, weapons centers and supply stations.

Most of them were smokers. They had a limited supply of cigarettes. After a few puffs they extinguished them and saved what was left for later. Apu, being a smoker as well, had a sizeable supply of cigarettes stored on the top shelf of the coat closet. One day, I decided that if I removed a pack once in a while, he probably wouldn't even notice. This method of "borrowing " cigarettes from Apu and giving them to the sentries opened the doors to real friendships. I knew that Apu would not be oblivious to the dwindling supply of cigarettes forever. He would surely question me in the near future, but I had no regrets about depleting his reserves. This was probably a subconscious act of revenge for the many years of having to inhale the dreaded smoke exhaled by my parents and their friends during the long hours of card games. Even today, as an adult, I don't understand the benefits of smoking. As a kid, I also figured that if we had to evacuate in a hurry, fewer cigarettes would take up less space in a backpack.

I had great compassion for these partisans who endangered their lives on a daily basis guarding our village. A few days earlier, keeping company with my partisan friend Pavel at the entrance to the town, I had a very special experience. He was telling me about his sleepless night due to an assignment he had to carry out with a couple of his buddies. He could barely keep his eyes open.

"Ondrejko ," he began, "will you help me out while I take a short nap under the tree over there?" He pointed to a shaded tree about ten feet up the hill behind us.

"What do you want me to do?" I asked.

"I want you to guard the road."

Guard the road? I couldn't believe what I had just heard. I was nine years old and he wanted me to guard the main road to Bobrovček? Granted, there was very little traffic, and I could, by that time, recognize most of the peasants, but still...

"What happens if some strangers come?"

"Here, take my rifle, lie down in the ditch behind the bank, and aim it towards the road," he explained, sounding a little bit nervous.

I had a good view of a long stretch of road ahead, but asked, "What do you want me to do if I see a soldier come by?"

"Call me, wake me up."

"What if you don't hear me?"

"Start shooting. That will wake me up. Aim and pull the trigger. Make sure the rifle butt rests on your shoulder."

"*Dobre.*" (Good.) I took my position and sat, tense and stiff with my pointer finger on the trigger, praying and hoping that nothing or no one would approach the village. Every couple of minutes, I looked back at the tree to make sure Pavel was still there, asleep. Five minutes passed, ten minutes passed, nothing happened. It was a nice, calm, sunny day. As I recall, only a shepherd boy walked by with a small flock of sheep. Finally, after almost half an hour, Pavel woke up and shouted, "Everything alright, Ondrejko?"

At this moment I realized that I was barely breathing. "*Všetko je v poriadku.*" (Everything is OK.) I yelled back at him. Oh, what a relief! My first attempt at soldiering. He walked back to me and patted me on the head. "Thanks, Ondrejko, good job. It wasn't so hard, ha?"

I was so proud of myself. But did I dare tell Anyu what I did? No. It might have upset her. This experience remained my secret. As hard as it was for me not to share everything with my parents, I kept this one to myself.

Once I had a frightening encounter in the village with a crazy dog. I was walking alone on our side of the creek – I seldom crossed over to the other side by myself – and suddenly, a mid-size dog started barking at me from across the creek. At first, I ignored it, but after a while I got annoyed. I lifted a small stone and pretended to throw it over the creek. I tried to shut it up, but it just kept on barking. I continued to walk home. Somehow, the nasty dog crossed the creek and I started to run. Of course, it caught up with me, determined to bite, so I lifted my legs high as I ran, but to no avail. The dog tried to bite my right leg from the back. Lucky for me, it only took a chunk out of my pants. At that moment, a couple of villagers came to my rescue and shooed the dog away. I was so upset and scared, I started to cry the minute I entered our house. My parents got scared too. I was mostly embarrassed about the whole thing. Too bad I couldn't keep that incident a secret. Growing up was not so easy.

CHAPTER 30

Escape to the Tatra Mountains

Every passing day grew colder. The trees were nearly bare and the ground was always covered with a thin layer of snow. News reports coming in from the Russian front were very encouraging, however. The Russians were crippling the German advance, especially their supply lines. The partisans told us that before long, Germany would have to surrender. In the meantime, the Slovak uprising which started in August in the town of Banska Bystrica, a city in central Slovakia surrounded by mountains, fizzled out. Many people were killed by the fighting and even more were arrested and shipped to slave labor and concentration camps. I didn't fully understand what all this meant, but I knew in my heart that these brave Slovak people would probably never be seen again. The fear I had of this happening to us gave me many nightmares.

Anyu and Apu were very concerned about the well-being of our relatives. Since we came to Bobrovček, we had lost track of family and friends. We didn't have access to telephones and could not imagine how and where they were. Most likely, like us, they were simply surviving day-to-day.

During this time, my parents wore two faces. One was happy, for public consumption outside the house, and the other somber, even sad, behind closed doors. I saw the change as we went in and out and I hurt terribly inside for their masquerade. I dared not say a thing, but I knew they were hurting inside.

One early afternoon in November, I went to visit my friend the partisan, Pavel, during his guard duty at the other end of the village. As always, he was happy to have company and a few new cigarettes. We spoke about all kinds of things with minimal distraction. Around three o'clock, we saw the shape of a horse and rider in the distance, galloping in our direction. Pavel turned to me, "When he gets nearer, I want you to sit behind that tree. He mustn't see you. Understand?"

Within a few minutes we both recognized the man on the horse. He was a partisan from Pavel's unit. He slowed down as he rode past and in a very loud, excited voice yelled, "Alert! Alert! Nazi soldiers entered the village of Bobrovec this morning! They're just a few miles away! We better clear our asses out, now! They can't be far!" Then he galloped furiously on into our village.

Pavel quickly slung his rifle over his shoulder and helped me up. This was the worst news any of us could have possibly heard.

"Oskar, you better run home and tell your parents," he advised. "Tell them it's time to clear out and fast. Nazi soldiers are only ten minutes from town. Be careful!" He hoisted his backpack and headed on to the road. I followed but could not keep up with him. He was way ahead of me when I reached our house.

"Anyu! Apu!" I yelled, bursting into the room, breathless. "The Nazis are in Bobrovec, just a few miles from here!"

"*Jaj, istenem!* (Oh my God!)," exclaimed Anyu. "We must get out as soon as possible. Frici, you and Osika start packing. I will run over to Blaza's house to alert their son Vilo about leading us in to the forest. I never thought it would be so soon!"

"Irenke," said Apu. "Hold on! Don't panic. We must wait. In daylight, some of the peasants might see us. How do you know they won't inform the Nazis that we city folk are hiding in the forest? We are much safer leaving under the cover of darkness. Let's not take any chances. Start packing and I'll be back in a few minutes."

We realized we could not walk into the mountains carrying suitcases. We tried our best to pack as much as possible into more portable rucksacks. We took non-perishable foods, medications, blankets, our warmest clothes and boots, toiletries, tools, twine, a sewing kit and a few other important items we thought we might need. We filled our pockets and carried small bags. We ate dinner in a hurry and, as soon as it turned dark, headed for the road, following the lead of Vilo who had agreed earlier to take us to the edge of the forest. From there, we were to find a shepherd's cabin further on. We followed a path that took us through some fields covered with light snow. A full moon hung overhead lighting the way. To our great surprise, in the distance ahead, we saw the silhouettes of another group of people heading towards the forest as well. I was terribly frightened. I imagined the worst.

"Don't worry, Osika," Anyu whispered. "They are most likely our own people who were hiding in Bobrovček without our knowledge. It's OK."

I took her hand and pressed closer, hoping she was right. But I kept looking back over my shoulder, praying silently that we were not being followed.

Tatra Mountains Panorama
Photo courtesy of www.PeterDobrovsky.sk

CHAPTER 31

In the Mountains

Every sound set my ears abuzz. Every rock or tree seemed an important landmark. Under a clear and starry sky, I was very alert to our surroundings, trying to remember the route we were taking toward the mountains in case we tried to return to Bobrovček. As I looked back, I could detect a few more shapes of people in the distance, walking on a different path. "It must be more people running from the Nazis," I said to my parents. They didn't seem worried. But I wondered who these people were, where they were coming from, and more important, where they were going.

Walking up a gradual incline slowed us down. It also meant we were ascending into forests growing on higher ground. Sure enough, as our breathing got harder, we found ourselves entering a dense grove of tall spruce trees. Vilo stopped. "This is as far as I can take you. I told my parents I'd be back in an hour."

"How do we find the shepherd's cabin?" asked Apu.

"Continue uphill on this path until you reach the creek and then follow it. It will lead you to a large meadow where you will see a few small cabins. It takes about two to three hours to get there. There'll be more snow on the ground the higher you go."

Apu gave him some money and thanked him for his help. He left and we continued on our own. Visibility was good. The light from the moon shone down through the treetops and on to the white snow lighting up the path. I was in the lead in spite of my fear. Anyu walked behind me and Apu behind her. Walking in the wilderness scared me but I tried not to show it. My parents were city people, having no prior experience of survival in the mountains, especially not in the winter. Our progress was slow due to the weight we were carrying and the uncertainty of the way. We spoke little, each absorbed in our own thoughts. Every few minutes we stopped to rest. The silence around us was deafening.

I wondered where my Slovak partisan friends had gone. Would I see them somewhere in the mountains? We had been walking for over an hour, uphill. Fatigue and hunger slowed us down, so we decided to stop and rest under a tree where the ground was flat and padded with dry pine needles. We cleared away the snow with our shoes, spread out a blanket, and sat down to eat sandwiches that Anyu had prepared before we left Bobrovček.

"It's getting very late," said Anyu. "We would be better off spending the night right here."

"Why not continue?" said Apu. "Wouldn't we be a lot more comfortable sleeping in a cabin?"

"Frici, we haven't even reached the creek. If we continue now it may take us half the night to find the meadow and the cabins. Possibly even longer. Let's just stay here and get an early start in the morning." And so we hunkered down for the night under a pine tree. Anyu said the *shemah* and laid down next to me. Apu snuggled in on the other side of her. I tried to close my eyes but realized that I was too scared of sleeping unprotected out in the wild. Every few minutes I opened my eyes and looked around in the dark. What if wild animals roamed here? Every little noise woke me up. I pretended to be asleep but could not manage it. The night passed slowly as I stayed close to Anyu. My toes were cold but the rest of me stayed warm. I kept hoping to see the sun rise and although exhausted, I kept quiet. I didn't want to disturb my parents who seemed to be sound asleep. At last, I finally detected a ray of sunlight tipping the tops of the trees and lighting up the forest floor. I lay quietly waiting for one of them to wake up.

Thank you, dear God for watching over us. I said my traditional morning prayer and got up. Within a few minutes, the entire forest was illuminated. The white snow and delicious smell of the pine-scented mountain air instantly erased my fear. I could hardly wait to get going into a new world of adventure. Following a quick breakfast, we gathered up our bags and got back on the path. Luck seemed to be on our side and the weather was perfect, somewhat chilly, but the sky was clear. We could hear our footsteps crunching in the snow. The three of us continued marching forward like a miniature army. Apu, however, needed to stop and catch his breath every fifteen or twenty minutes or so. He carried the heaviest load. My poor Apu was not used to being a beast of burden.

By midday, we heard the trickle of water. I looked down into a ravine on the right and saw a stream. "Anyu, Apu, look, look! Down below is the creek that Vilo told us to follow."

A few yards further up on our left, nestled among the trees, was a small log cabin. "*Danke got* !" (Thank God!") exclaimed Apu in German. He was really tired. He could hardly wait to lie down and take a rest. He admitted earlier that he had barely slept the night before. He was chilled and uncomfortable on the ground, so it turned out I wasn't the only one who didn't sleep. Anyu told us she tried to stay awake in order to watch over us. It appears we all failed our first test in the mountains.

We stopped on the trail and observed the surroundings, apprehensive about approaching the cabin. It should have been vacant because the shepherds never brought their flocks up this high during winter. When they did, they didn't even lock the cabin doors. A few minutes passed; no sign of life. We got closer, stopped and watched. Nothing moved, no sounds at all. We walked up to the door and knocked. No answer. We waited.

"Halo, Halo!" Anyu called out. Still no response. Apu tried the door latch. Nothing happened. We were about to leave when the door opened slowly. A middle-aged woman appeared. "What do you want?" she asked suspiciously in Slovak.

Anyu explained who we were and asked if we could please join her. "We have a nine-year-old son. He is a good child, won't bother anyone. We are able to share expenses. I will be happy to cook meals..."

"We don't have room for anyone else in here," she answered.

"We can sleep on the floor," my mother offered. Then a man walked up and began to close the door. "Sorry, you'll have to find a place somewhere else," he insisted coldly.

"Do you know of another cabin nearby?" Anyu asked.

"We were told that higher up in the mountains are two cabins close to each other. There are other Jewish people living in them. Just follow the creek for about two hours. Good luck." And he shut the door.

Apu fumed, shaking his fist. "Shame on you! What kind of Jews are you?"

We had no choice but to continue our journey upwards. Hopefully, we would find the cabins before nightfall. Once we started gaining altitude, Apu's breathing grew heavier. He had always enjoyed good food and good music in the city. He was a fine musician, a trained violinist and therefore, not in the best physical condition to climb a mountain. One of the items he was carrying, in fact, was his violin in a hard, black case. I could tell that my dear Apu was going to have a hard time getting around in this environment. We made several stops to rest and eat, but we had to push on before it got too late. The thought of another night in the wilderness was not welcome.

CHAPTER 32

A Wilderness Cabin

We entered the next forested area by mid-afternoon and just past a large clearing found another cabin, somewhat larger than the one we were turned away from. The people we met there were much more friendly and welcoming. They responded affirmatively to our request. "We will manage," they said. "Come in and rest." We were ecstatic and grateful.

"What's your name little boy?" asked one of the strangers, looking at me.

"My parents call me Osi. My real name is Oskar." Relieved, I could be called by my real name again. I looked around, surveying the interior. The cabin was built entirely of wood. Opposite the entry door I could see two levels of bunk beds the length of the back wall. Each of the side walls had a small glass window. To the right stood a table with several chairs around it and to the left was an old, black, pot-bellied stove with a large pot resting on top. A pile of dry, chopped up branches lay in front of the stove. A tall, narrow pipe extended up from the stove through the roof to the outside. This relic served as the heating system and cooking stove for all the inhabitants of the cabin.

We were assigned an upper-level bunk to sleep, the three of us together. I counted around twelve people in this small space. It seemed there was a second cabin nearby, also fully occupied by Jewish people. Neither had electricity or running water. Water had to be carried in from the narrow creek in the ravine. People relieved themselves in the surrounding forest. That did not present a problem because everything froze overnight. Any food refuse was left in the woods to be consumed by wild animals roaming the area. I heard that bears lived in these forests as well, but so far, no one had come across one. I hoped I wouldn't run into a bear.

It took a long time to get used to this new life with strangers. There were many problems. First, no one had a single moment of privacy. Second, our sleeping space was so tight that when one of us needed to turn the other way, we all had to change direction. Third, if I woke up at night needing to urinate, I had to walk outside into the cold darkness which was uncomfortable and scary. The only exception among us who did not go outside was an older man whose health was failing. He urinated into a pot in the corner of the room. The noise woke me up many a night.

For the sake of peace, a set of rules regulated our daily activities. Sign-up lists were posted on the wall for nighttime guard duty, collection of firewood, use of the stove-top for preparation of meals, water carriers from the creek to the cabin, and a number of other functions for the benefit of all.

As winter progressed, new challenges had to be overcome. Major snow-storms dumped huge drifts of heavy snow around us, often blocking the door. On some occasions, we couldn't get out for several days. When the temperature dropped below freezing, the cabin became like an icebox. Wearing all our clothes and using all of our blankets did not stop us from shivering. My parents and I had to squeeze tightly against each other and utilize our body heat to keep from freezing.

Luckily, the spells of extreme weather were short in duration. Two major concerns were always on our minds —our health and the timely resupply of food. Thus far, the young peasant who had previously been hired by the current residents of the cabin to bring food stuffs and random supplies for all of us had shown up on time, once-a-week. When he came, he also kept everyone up-to-date on the progress of the war between the Nazis and the Russian forces, as well as the living conditions in the valley below. Things were tough for the villagers and many townsfolk suffered casualties. Our young courier was paid handsomely for his services since his secret trips delivering food to us were illegal and carried a stiff punishment. He was always reminded not to disclose our location in the forest to anyone, no matter what. He assured us he would always be very careful and closed-mouthed about his trips.

Almost a month had passed since we arrived. I figured out how to keep busy and get out from under the feet of the adults who often grumbled and complained. Everyone's mood was much better during sunny days, but we had to beware when heavy clouds darkened the skies. Some of our cabin dwellers fell into obvious depression. Outbursts of anger and crying spells were common. We had tense moments when someone very sad gave up and threatened to commit suicide. This affected everyone deeply. Some others decided that life was not worth living and it was preferable to go down to the valley and surrender to the Nazis! We were all at risk if someone would indeed give him or herself up. Apu said that through torture, the Hlinka Guardists or the Nazi officials could make someone give up our secret hiding place and get us all killed. We couldn't let that happen.

More and more, I kept myself at a safe distance from the cabin. My hatchet was a helpful tool for gathering dry firewood. That became a wonderful excuse for me to stay outside for longer periods of time. I came to the conclusion, however, that one day our luck would run out. A hunter or an army patrol or even a lost skier might inadvertently or purposely expose us. I didn't want to be caught in a surprise roundup.

Anyu told me repeatedly that if we were caught, I should try to run away and get back to Bobrovček to our nice landlords. "They will take good care of you," she said. "I am sure of it." I wasn't so sure.

I took over the job of maintaining a continuous fire in the stove. First, I was allowed to do so on a trial basis. When everyone saw I was doing a good job, I was appointed official "keeper of the fire." My new responsibility kept me busy all day, every day. At night, whoever was the appointed *shomer* (guard) saw to the task of stoking the fire.

Otherwise, a typical day went like this: If I wore pajamas to sleep, the first thing I did after I woke up was get dressed which included putting on boots and a warm coat and hat. Brushing teeth, washing hands and face and relieving myself had to be done outside. We kept boiled water on the stove for hot drinks. Once a week, preferably on sunny days, we washed each other's backs with soap outside, using ice cold water from the creek. If the creek was frozen, a handful of snow would do the job. Anyu did a great job washing my back. At first the cold water burned my skin, but as she continued to rub, my skin warmed up and retained the heat under my shirt and sweater for a long time. Whenever possible, if there was ample hot water in the big pot on the stove, I snuck out a cupful and washed myself with soap.

Another reason for having enough hot water sitting on the stove at all times was to serve our occasional visitors, the partisans. Higher up, above us in the mountains, lived a unit of clandestine resistance fighters. During their free time, some of them enjoyed visiting us. They dropped in unannounced, primarily during daytime hours, and usually one at a time. We always welcomed them with open arms. We felt safe knowing that they were in the vicinity. Of course, they did not ever disclose their hideout locations. Besides, they never stayed very long at any of them.

Most of the partisans were Russians. Their average age was early twenties, the commanders somewhat older. No one in our cabin spoke Russian, however there were some similarities between our language and theirs. The women in our cabin always fed them. Not surprisingly, they were often more interested in drinking alcoholic beverages.

In addition to the Russians, we had also been visited by Czech, Slovak and Yugoslav freedom fighters. In general, they were nice young people but, as in any group, just one bad apple could spoil a good lot. They were all aware that Nazi forces in the region were continuing efforts to capture and deport Jewish people, resistance fighters and political enemies.

One incident caused us great pain. One afternoon, a partisan we called "Boris, the Russian", burst into the cabin and informed us that Nazi soldiers were on their way up.

"Go hide in the rocks," he shouted. Panic ensued and people ran in all directions, including us. When the cabin emptied out, Boris helped himself to a couple bottles of wine that we used sparingly for sacramental purposes on Friday evening's Shabbat *kiddush* and also to make *havdalah*, the service marking the end of the Sabbath.

We all returned slowly to the cabin when we realized that Boris's warning didn't materialize. The next day, on Friday, after the women lit the Shabbat candles and the men were about to make the blessing over the wine, the discovery was made that two bottles of the sacramental wine were missing. Boris disappeared from the scene and never returned. I was terribly disappointed. Up until then, in my eyes, all the partisans had been heroes.

High Tatras Shepherds Cabin
Photo courtesy of Ivan Kmit
@ivankmit_photography

CHAPTER 33

The Partisans

Our supplies dwindled slowly. We had no way to replenish the stolen wine. As other partisans visited us, our hospitality and generosity toward them lessened. The adults advised not to mention the theft to them.

"The partisan, Boris, must have had a drinking problem. Let's not anger him for he might become violent," said Anyu. Not long after this incident, my trust in all these fighters was shattered. Thanks to one man, however, it was soon revived. One of the regional commanders, Mikhail, came to us for recovery. He had been wounded during a firefight and had a bullet lodged in his right thigh. The pain was constant, but he handled it bravely. I felt sorry for him because he would have to endure a lot of discomfort until his troop found a surgeon in one of the local towns and could take him there —that is, a surgeon willing to risk his own safety to remove the bullet from Mikhail's thigh.

I was trying to be of help to him and he was very nice to me. He asked me to sit on his good leg so he could show me a photograph of his family. He had a pretty wife and two children in Russia. He kept telling me that I reminded him of his son who was my age. Our conversation was frustrating when we didn't understand each other's language. Meanwhile, he let me take apart his automatic weapon's magazine and play with the short, squat bullets, all thirty-two of them. I sat them up on the table just like I used to line up the miniature soldiers in our store in Prešov. On one end of the table was a row of Russian soldiers. Then came the battle and all the Nazi soldiers were flung off the table. Commander Mikhail applauded.

Two days and two nights later he was picked up by two partisans and carried off. Everyone wished him good luck. After a handshake and a pat on the head, he turned at the door and said in Russian, "*Spasiba.*" (Thanks. Everything will be alright.)

I became very sad after he left. For the next few days, I focused on maintaining the lookout bunker I made in the snow on a nearby hill. With every passing day, I realized the safety of our group was in many ways my responsibility, something I took very seriously. One morning, I detected the sound of an engine. At first, I thought it was a motorized vehicle on the opposite mountain. But then I spotted a light, single engine airplane flying slowly over the mountain, as if spying, searching for signs of life down in the forests. It was probably hoping to find partisans or refugees, while sowing fear among those who lived in the valley. It occurred to me right then that I better put out the fire in the stove to stop the smoke from escaping into the air. That would be a sure sign to the pilot that he needed to alert his command to investigate this area which would have been a calamity for us. We could all have been captured by Nazi soldiers.

The flyovers became more and more frequent. The peasant delivering food warned us about heightened patrol of mountain access roads by Nazi units. He changed the route he took every time he came up. He seemed to grow more tense and more worried as time went on. Pooling our resources, we had been paying him extra, hoping to encourage his continued interest in delivering food to us. If he quit, we would have all been in big trouble.

One night, I was awakened by the sound of rifle shots. At first, I got scared, imagining an assault by the Nazis on the partisans' headquarters. The shooting lasted about ten minutes, eventually disappearing into the distant valleys. We never found out what happened, but over the next few weeks the visits by the partisans ceased. My guess is they had to change the location of their headquarters after the firefight.

The intense cold and heavy snow forced me to spend more and more time indoors. Cloudy and snowy weather kept the spotter plane from frequent flyovers as well. For a number of days, I was not even able to collect firewood because of the height of the snowfall. My parents dared not let me go out. They were afraid I might get stuck somewhere in a deep snow drift, unable to even call for help.

Staying in the cabin for long stretches of time bored me terribly. I tried to keep busy drawing pictures, practicing Hebrew by reading in the siddur, playing cards, rereading one of my few story books, inventing and writing my own story, carving figures out of wood with my pocketknife, and helping Anyu wash clothes. I also did things for other people in our cabin. By chance, I got a new friend to play with, although she was three years younger than me and a girl, and I lacked patience playing with little girls.

She arrived by chance one morning, traveling with her parents from Poland. The three of them were in hiding for a long time in a village on the Polish side of the Tatra Mountains near the city of Zakopane. Their hideout was compromised and the only thing left for them to do was cross the mountains to Slovakia. Since Poland was teeming with Nazi operatives they had no choice but to walk in the snow and cold for two weeks straight. Miraculously, they found our cabin and told us the details of their escape and wandering through the mountains. The story seemed impossible, but it was true. They practically begged us to let them stay in our cabin. After hearing how they survived and made such a courageous escape, no one had the heart to turn them away.

It became really crowded in such a small space but we managed. My parents and the Polish couple hit it off. Anyu commented that their experiences in Poland would serve us well here. The husband was a real survivor, very smart and strong; he carried his little girl on his back through most of their hike through the Tatras. His wife seemed to be a pleasant, agreeable woman.

Anyu shared with me some of his concerns regarding our vulnerability in case of a surprise sweep of the mountains by the Nazi military. He suggested an emergency plan be put in place for just our family and theirs. Anyu and the Polish man went for a walk uphill, deeper into the forest, to look for an alternative hiding place. When they returned, Anyu told Apu and me, quietly and discretely, that they discovered a small cave carved into a huge boulder, large enough to accommodate the six of us in a sitting position.

"Let us hope we won't need to use the *jaskyňa* (cave)," said Anyu in Slovak, "but it's good to know we have another place to hide."

December arrived on the wings of a powerful snowstorm. For nearly a week, the heavy snow fell continuously all day and through the night, accompanied by mournful, howling winds that intensified by morning. The eerie sound of that wind whistling around our cabin frightened me and I had a hard time falling asleep at night, especially when the entire cabin shook and creaked. In addition, we had an extremely hard time maintaining the fire in the stove. The wind blew in through the narrow chimney and extinguished the fire repeatedly. It seemed like the relentless winter wanted to kill us all.

On top of that, at the same time, we had another setback. Our food supply delivery was late. Everyone blamed the inclement weather. First, we counted the tardiness in hours, then in days. Some of us were getting worried. As another day passed and still no sign of the peasant-boy. Hunger made people edgy. As time went on, our mood became very somber. People became secretive about their personal reserves of non-perishables. Speculation as to what happened to our delivery boy entered everyone's mind. We wondered what could have happened to him. Every few hours, someone walked over from the other cabin to check on the situation. Then, someone else from our cabin volunteered to check on them. This useless traffic went on for several days.

Rumors started flying back and forth. More frequent arguments flared up. The tension inside our cabin felt like a smoldering fire. A wrong word could cause it to ignite. The men had been discussing ways to find sources of food if the peasant did not show up within four or five more days. With no way to hunt, how long could we go on?

In spite of some serious belt-tightening, everyone's supplies were dwindling rapidly. Ideas ranged from the ridiculous to drastic. "If we don't do something quickly, we are going to die from starvation," said one couple, or "Someone will have to go to a village, break into a house, and steal some food," said another, or "We may have to give ourselves up to the Nazis."

Another voice was heard. "A couple of the men should take Osika to the edge of Bobrovček and let him sneak into the village to a peasant's house to ask for food."

Anyu spoke up in anger. "Oh no you won't! I am not going to endanger our son. He stays right here. Do you hear me, Osika? Don't you dare leave with anyone!"

The final outcome was a daring plan, attempted one night. Two of the youngest men in our group decided to hike down to the valley and rob a peasant family of their food. They left about an hour before dark with empty rucksacks on their backs. Both cabins fell into total silence as they waited. For several hours, no one spoke. Finally, a voice was heard. "What a stupid idea! If they get caught by the police or by soldiers, we are all in trouble. God forbid, if they are tortured, our hiding place will be compromised."

It was midnight when they finally returned. We were all happy to see them back again, unharmed, but the mission had failed completely. They said the valley was swarming with patrols of Nazi soldiers and Hlinka Guardists. They couldn't find a single chance to sneak into the village. They returned empty-handed, extremely discouraged and embarrassed, as well as cold, wet and exhausted.

Their failure was my gain since no one spoke further about trying to enter the village. I was especially relieved since some of the adults had so boldly dared suggest that I should go and steal some food. Hungry as I was, as we all were, I couldn't imagine such a risk. The very idea terrified me. In truth, I dared not complain, even to Anyu, about that idea or any other. But I couldn't deny that I had started to miss home and our former life in Prešov, life before the roundups started, with a consistent ache in my nine-year-old heart. Not just home, but the sound of Apu's joyful violin and the friendly customers in our store, the rich aromas of Anyu's mouth-watering cooking on Shabbat, the comfort of my own soft bed, and even the warm, endearing hugs from my beloved grandparents. So many things I took for granted, all taken from me now. These things seemed very far away now, like a dream from long ago. Memories filled my thoughts as I lay by my parents' side at night, taking me back to another time of safety and security, but they also made me sad, making me wonder when we might finally be free and this nightmare would come to its end.

Winter in the High Tatras
Photo: 3D_generator

CHAPTER 34

On the Edge of Disaster

December 25, 1944.

I will never forget this day. One of the partisans who had been visiting us frequently, Volodya, entered our cabin shortly before noon and made an announcement that a Nazi military unit had been observed earlier searching our mountains in a combing formation. He advised us to disperse and seek shelter or find a hiding place somewhere else and fast! This was devastating news. Blank faces exchanged somber glances. After he left, a discussion erupted, "Don't listen to him. They are trying to trick us again. It's all about the wine. As soon as we leave, they'll sneak into the cabin and help themselves to it."

"Agreed. Let's not fall for their evil deception."

"We are staying put. We are not going anywhere."

I looked to my parents for guidance. Anyu looked exasperated, her lips set in a grim line, her arms crossed before her defiantly. "We'd better leave," she said after a few moments of deliberation. Then she added a sharp tilt of her head, as if to say, "Let's go." The Polish family had already left. We quickly followed in their footsteps, catching up to them.

The day was cold and cloudy. Frozen patches on the snow made it hard to walk uphill. We walked single file, led by the Polish man whose name I have long forgotten, his little girl, his wife, and then Anyu and Apu. I was last, as usual, pulling a pine branch behind me to erase our footsteps in the snow, a trick I invented.

Apu struggled, weighted down by a full, heavy rucksack. He carried his walking cane in his right hand, a hat covering his head. About fifteen minutes into our climb along a narrow, frozen ridge, we saw a sharp drop on our right side into a deep ravine cut by a narrow creek. I slowed down due to Apu's difficulty in climbing up the steep incline. With great effort, he almost made it to the top when suddenly, he lost his footing, falling sideways over the edge of the ravine, and began to tumble downward, down the slick side of the mountain. I got a brief glimpse of him only to see a horrifying picture—his body seemed to bounce up and down as it tumbled with the rucksack on his back, his hat rolling along above his head and his cane sliding along beside. At first I was in shock, I could not believe what I saw, and then I began to scream, "Anyu, Anyu, Anyu!"

My mother turned her head to see what was the matter and I pointed to where Apu had just disappeared beyond the ridge."*Apu spadol!*" (*Apu fell down!*) I shouted in Slovak over and over. Anyu hurried over and the two of us ran to the precipitous edge. We both stood and watched Apu's long, uncontrollable fall toward what we feared might be his very end until he disappeared from our sight. Anyu shouted, "Frici, Frici, try to stop yourself!"

But Apu could not break his fall. Within seconds, he had disappeared into the dark depths of the steep ravine. We could not see any trace of him. All was deathly silent. We stood motionless in despair, hearing no response to our calls. I was shaking from head to toe, incredulous at what had just happened. "Apu! Apu! Answer us!"

The Polish family approached. "Is he alright?"

Anyu had no answer. All we could do was continue to desperately call his name. "Frici, Apu, Frici, Are you still alive?" My mother called out, nearly hysterical.

The Polish man took her arm. "Iréna, we have to keep going before the Nazis find us here. He is probably gone. It is too late."

Anyu turned toward him, eyes blazing, "No! We don't know that! We must help him! We cannot leave him behind. Please, help me find him. Please! Come down the hill with me. I cannot do it alone."

The Polish man looked at his wife and daughter in distress.

"I am begging you, please help us!" pleaded Anyu again.

Finally the man's wife said to him in Polish, "*Chodž!*" (*Go.*)

Hand-in-hand, the two carefully descended the steep hill and disappeared into the abyss-like darkness. The Pole's wife, his daughter and I stood motionless, waiting for some sound to come from the forest below. I was sobbing silently, expecting the very worst. Every couple of minutes, I shouted, "Anyu, Apu," hoping to get an answer. Straining my eyes to catch some movement, I finally detected what looked like a few people inching their way up the hill. After about thirty minutes, I saw Apu, struggling to stand, assisted by Anyu and the Polish man, limping to the top of the ridge towards us. I stopped sobbing. God performed a miracle. Apu is alive.

We reassembled. With Apu practically being carried by my mother and the Polish man, we headed out once more. My father seemed dazed and weak. Our procession continued slowly for about an hour before we arrived at the opening to the cave. Apu was in terrible pain, moaning, his leg probably broken, we couldn't be too sure. With great effort, we all squeezed into the opening and seated ourselves on a blanket spread out on the cave floor. We tried to make Apu as comfortable as we could, grateful he had no other apparent injuries.

A light snow had started to fall. As I was about to enter the cave, an idea popped into my head. I walked over to a pine tree growing nearby, chopped off two large bushy branches with my hatchet, and carried them to the cave in a circuitous path. Before I proceeded to enter, I made sure that all the footprints were cleared away. I backed into the mouth of the cave, pulling the two branches with my two hands, and propped them up vertically like trees, covering the cave's entrance. I figured if I couldn't see out, no one could see the cave opening either unless they removed the branches.

As I settled down, I suddenly noticed a young woman to my left side I had not seen before. She told me she was a partisan, and her name was Anička. She got separated from her partisan unit and became lost in the forest. Unbeknownst to us, she had been following us on our way up, right behind an older man who lived in the other cabin. While I was chopping down the pine branch, she and the old man pushed themselves into the cave. That's why it had become so tight that almost no one could move.

In a way, I was happy she was here with us because she carried a weapon. She was a fighter. The old man parked himself at the other end of the cave next to the Polish family. One small thing worried me a lot, however. The old man had a cold and coughed every few minutes. I shared my concern with Anyu and she spoke to the Polish man about it who shook his head and assured us that he would keep an eye on the elder member of our group and help him control his coughing as best he could.

CHAPTER 35

Saved by a Cave

I felt very fortunate that we had all made it this far. Especially, I was thankful to the Almighty that Apu was still with us. Only an hour earlier, I thought we had lost him. Miraculously, he escaped tragedy with only some kind of severe leg injury. Only time would tell since we certainly couldn't take him to a doctor. Anyu told me that they found him just short of the creek, against a large rock, motionless, and in shock. Since his return, he had not said anything about the fall except complain about the terrible pain. Anyu helped him swallow a couple of aspirin which she luckily brought with us.

In the cave, the rule was total silence. Once in a while, someone whispered something. The old man tried to muffle his coughs. As I peeked through the branches, I saw large snowflakes falling. By then, it was close to three in the afternoon. Thus far, all remained quiet around us. Whispered conversations sifted through the cave from time-to-time. Anyu leaned over, seeking advice from the Polish man. "How long do you think we should stay here?"

"Until nighttime," he replied, in a reassuring voice.

The partisan girl next to me whispered, "The Nazis are afraid to come up to the mountains at night because we have the upper hand in the dark. They don't know where we are." Only a few minutes later however, promptly at three o'clock, the silence was broken by several loud gunshots, followed by screams and harsh, male voices giving orders coming from the direction of the cabins.

"*Raus juden, raus juden, schnel, schnel!*" (Get out Jews! Get out Jews! Quickly! Quickly!)

We heard many voices in German and Slovak, plus the sound of men, women and babies crying, and more gunshots. Each one caused me to shudder, and a chill ran up my spine. Then a woman's shrill voice shouted, "*Nicht schiesen bitte, kleine kinder sindt da!*" (Please don't shoot, we have little children here!)

By now, we were all shaking and had reached for each other. I held Anyu's hand with my right, but Anička, on my left side, refused to take my left hand. Later I understood why.

Our nerves were stretched like rubber bands. I heard Anyu whisper in Hungarian "*Istenem, segits nekünk.*" (God help us!) The shooting stopped as suddenly as it had begun. No more loud noises came from below. Then we smelled smoke in the air. Someone asked in a whisper, "What? Are they burning down the forest? What are we going to do?"

The thought came to my mind that they might spread out and search the area. I peeked out, looking for fire. I could not see anything or anyone. Ten minutes went by. I heard something resembling the crunch of footsteps in the snow. They were coming closer. Someone whispered again, "Do you hear footsteps?"

Then, "*Csit-csak !*" Anyu warned us.

I detected the distinct sounds of heavy boots against rock and frozen snow. I didn't smell smoke anymore, but I did smell danger. Did someone see us entering the cave? If so, we were in big trouble. Trapped! Then we heard distinct voices. It sounded like two men talking to each other in German. I could feel Anička reaching for her pistol. Anyu took my hand again. It was shaking. A total hush fell over the cave. The two Germans were walking in circles right outside our entrance. They were searching for something or somebody. My heart was racing. I closed my eyes and said a prayer. *Please God, don't let them find us.* I was sure everyone around me was doing the same.

I kept staring at the pine branches spread across the opening, hoping they would not move. *Pán Božko drahy* I prayed again in Slovak, please make the soldiers go away from here and keep the old man from coughing. A strange sensation crept under my butt; I felt warm liquid seeping through my pants, coming from my left. I didn't dare move or say anything at this awkward moment. In the meantime, while I was distracted, the conversation outside grew fainter. The soldiers had moved on.

Anička squeezed my trembling hand, leaned over, and whispered in my ear, "I am so sorry, I couldn't hold it anymore." I instinctively moved closer to my mother, away from the puddle of urine. Soon, silence returned to the forest around us. But we were still afraid to move. Had they left the area or were they hiding nearby, hoping to catch more Jews or partisans?

And so, remaining cautious and vigilant, we spent the next twelve hours in the cave, overnight, in the bitter cold, eagerly awaiting the light of day. I woke up as soon as dawn peeked through the branches. My pants were still wet under the left cheek. Anička was fast asleep, snoring. Anyu, of course, woke up when I bent forward to look out.

Everyone wanted to know what I could see.

"Trees and snow," was my answer. "Lots of trees and snow." It didn't take long though, before we heard a distant whistle. This time I peeked out and saw a person walking at a distance, coming in our direction. The whistling grew louder. The old man with us suddenly spoke up, "That's my son! He must be looking for me!" Desperately wanting to get out of the cave, he started to push.

The Polish man held him back. "Stay put! This might be a trick. The Nazis may have captured him and now they are using him to lead them to you. Let's keep quiet until we are sure that he is alone. Osika, see if there is anyone else walking with him."

I looked out again, straining my eyes. The man just kept walking up the hill, looking around and whistling a specific tune used by his family, an old Slavic tradition. I reported back that I didn't see anyone else walking with him or behind him. The old man grew very anxious.

"Please, let me out!" he insisted. "My Tibi took off with the partisans and left me behind. That's why I followed you here. He is trying to find me." He crawled over everyone to get to the cave opening. The Polish man told him to answer his son's whistle, which he did several times. Tibi followed the sound and walked straight to our cave. "*Otec, kde si?*" he said in Slovak. (Father, where are you?)

"I am here, inside," answered the old man. At this point, he pushed through the branches and stood up to embrace his son. Then his son kneeled down and briefly filled us in on the events of the day before.

"It was terrifying," he began. "I was hiding in the trees and saw the soldiers with guns surround both cabins, then start shooting bullets in the air, and shouting "Jews, get out!" At first nobody exited, so they kicked in the doors and started dragging people outside, one-by-one. Before they left with everyone in a line, a few soldiers spread out and searched the area thoroughly. I was lucky they didn't find me. Meanwhile, they set fire to the two cabins and marched everyone down the mountain, on in to Bobrovček. That's all I know."

Anyu shook her head in disbelief. wiping the tears from her eyes, "May God protect them," she sighed, "and save their souls." Then she hugged me tight and kissed my cheek, grateful we were all safe. Apu said a prayer, quietly, in Hebrew, then added, "Osi, it was very wise of you to cover the cave opening with branches. That brilliant idea may have saved us, one and all."

That day I felt very proud.

Winter in the High Tatras
Photo courtesy of: Ivan Kmit
@ivankmit_photography

CHAPTER 36

Finding a New Place to Hide

We were all relieved to hear that no one actually got hurt, but who knew what was the fate of those who were captured, what horrible things happened after they were taken away? We all had visions of people being shot when we heard the terrible screaming and pleading. We were only to learn much later that some had actually been spared.

Tibi and the old man, his father, said goodbye, wished us good luck, and left. While we were talking to Tibi however, Anička snuck out and took off without saying a single word. I was hurt and disappointed by her. She had protected us in a way, and I even rested my head on her shoulder while we slept. She appeared out of nowhere and then disappeared into the wild, as suddenly as she had arrived.

At that point, there were just six of us left. I wondered what would happen next. The adults discussed new strategies. The Polish man thought we needed to go looking for a new spot to hide so we set out for higher ground, walking uphill along the creek. Within a short while, we saw a sharp indent in a sheer mountain wall, as if someone had cut into the hill with a knife. The indent seemed like a good possibility for hiding if we could only make some kind of cover. It had a clear view of the mountain on the other side of a deep ravine and a nearby road had been cut into the mountainside. With my 20/20 eyesight and thankfully, my good hearing, I, the unofficial guardian, would be able to monitor any traffic on the road.

We all agreed that we should erect some sort of structure at this location. The adults, minus Apu who could hardly walk, went down to the destroyed cabins to try to salvage what was left from the fire. In the meantime, I was told to cut down thick, dry branches, strong enough to be used for a frame. Before long, I had a whole pile of sturdy branches gathered near the rocky wall. About two hours later, the scouting party returned with what they could find— a roll of tar paper, a ball of brown string, a hammer, and a couple of partially full sacks of potatoes, beans, and frozen peas that were thankfully buried in the snow near the cabins which were still partially intact.

We went to work right away building a lean-to, using the sheer wall as the anchor. By the end of the day, we had a primitive structure with a roof over our heads. We even designed an exit door, secured from the inside with twine. The lean-to was approximately four feet high. I could stand straight up in it. The adults needed to bend down to enter and then, could only sit on the ground. Inside, they got around by crawling on all fours. The width measured about ten feet and the depth, around five. At night I could stretch out my legs, but the adults could not. They had to sleep with their knees bent.

The next morning, the scouting party went back to the burned-out cabins. This time they came back carrying the pot-belly stove —a grueling three-hour trip. With my pocket knife, I cut a hole in the tar paper roof to accommodate the round, black tin chimney. It ruined the blade. I could never clean it after that because of the sticky tar.

Each night, before I fell asleep, I often worried that something like a rock might fall off the top of the sheer mountain wall above and kill someone. Thank God it never happened.

The six of us now occupied this flimsy shelter, cut off and isolated from humanity. We were totally on our own. Our survival hinged on our ability to manage our meager resources, subsisting on limited food intake like bean soup or a meager slice of potato. Most of all, we relied on sheer willpower to cope with the hardships we still had to overcome, such as our own personal health issues and whatever else Mother Nature doled out in the way of snowstorms, cold temperatures, bone-chilling wind and wild animals. Plus, there was always the danger of betrayal by occasional hunters passing through the wilderness, or by a military patrol on foot or in the air.

Wanting to do my share, I created a lookout post for myself, an old tree stump, next to a larger pine tree that provided 180-degree visibility. The tree stump allowed me to sit comfortably or hide behind it if necessary. I surrounded it with packed snow, shoulder-high. The distance to the lean-to was anywhere between 30 to 50 steps, depending on the snow depth. Some mornings, the drifts were so high, we could not open the lean-to's flimsy door. Occasionally, we found ourselves snowed in for two to three days at a time. I tried to continue doing my job of collecting firewood and maintaining the fire in the pot-belly stove as best I could. If it went out, I could only light it by striking two flint-like rocks we found in the shepherd's cabin and took with us until I got a spark. All I can say is, we felt extremely fortunate that from December of 1944 to March of 1945, four long and difficult winter months, we stayed alive, maintaining our freedom and staying out of the hands of the murderous Nazis and their Slovak collaborators.

CHAPTER 37

Terrors in the Night

One night we had a terrible scare. We were awakened from our sleep by some strange grunts and squeals outside of our lean-to. The sounds resembled noises produced by the pigs in Bobrovček. The Polish man identified them as the grunts of wild hogs or boars. These animals could be very vicious. The scariest moments were seeing the tar paper cover being pushed inward. I was afraid they might break through! When we started clapping our hands, they backed off. We would be in grave danger if these animals succeeded to penetrate the tar paper walls. We had no weapons to protect ourselves. I don't believe my hatchet would have deterred them from attacking me or anyone else. The wild hog's intrusion that night added to my chronic anxiety and further affected my sleep, already suffering from our difficult circumstances.

In addition to my regular chores, I became the "water boy". As needed, we melted snow after a fresh storm and used it for cooking and drinking. In the absence of clean, fresh snow, I had to take a container with me down to the creek, fill it, and carry it back uphill, about 200 feet on a steep incline. That was hard work for a boy. I felt proud when I made it back to the top without help from anyone.

On really cold days, the creek froze. Sometimes my hatchet cut through the ice, other times I had to give up and return empty-handed. An element of risk was involved in descending the way down to the creek. The steep wall leading to the water was void of trees and clearly visible from the dirt road across the narrow valley which separated the two mountains. Before we went to the creek for water, we had to make sure the road was deserted. I had seen human beings on the road only twice since we arrived there, both times on sunny days. The first sighting was of two hunters walking with rifles, going north, apparently having a lively, animated discussion. The second time, I spotted members of a mountain army patrol in snow-white uniforms on skis, also heading north. The white uniforms made it hard to keep track of them against the white mountain in the background. Luckily, our lean-to was difficult to see from afar. Our provisions were always covered with snow and the walls were well camouflaged with pine branches.

Starting in mid-January, the frequency of air patrols increased. Almost every day when I heard the *put-put* noise of an engine belonging to a small propeller plane getting louder and louder, I ran into our shelter and quickly smothered the fire in the stove. This interfered with food preparation, however. Pouring water on the fire soaked the wood. When the danger of the flyovers ended, I had to remove the wet branches and replace them with dry ones. Often, we couldn't restart the fire until the next day.

One afternoon we had surprise visitors. A man and a woman, older than us, bundled up in warm clothes—Slovak Jews, lost and wandering in the mountains. They approached us and begged us to take them in. We did. We felt sorry for them and after all, Jews take care of each other.

Since relocating to the new shelter, time dragged on, making each day seem longer than the next. The adults were less active and spent more time inside, primarily because of the inclement weather, the deep snowpack, and the icy patches. By stabilizing it, Apu's leg was healing quite well, although he was not yet able to walk around outside. Of course, we all had to go out when nature called. We had no choice in this matter, so we helped him when necessary.

I dreaded having to drop my pants to relieve myself, especially on very cold days. In the cabins, we had coarse tissue paper or newsprint we used to wipe with. Here, we did not have that sort of luxury. When I was done, I grabbed a handful of snow and washed my behind with it. We got used to all sorts of changes and discomforts. But my mind constantly fantasized, created situations, and looked for solutions. My most creative invention was a wilderness-sort-of toilet.

I did not like to squat down with a naked behind. I could not control the position very well, especially with snow on the ground. Time after time, I fell backwards into the ice-cold snow. So, I came up with a design that would eliminate that shocking and uncomfortable event. I searched and found two trees growing very close to each other. I chopped down a thick, dry branch, smoothed it out, and tied each end to a tree with strong twine. In addition, I drove a nail salvaged from the burnt-out cabin, under the end of the branch so it could not slide down. As I built it for myself, I measured the height of the "seat" to suit me. After that, when I had to go, I didn't have to worry anymore. I could sit comfortably on the wooden "seat," holding on to the trees on each side with my hands.

A good thing, of course, did not go unnoticed. When my parents discovered my invention, I received my first order to build a prototype for the adults. This, however, was more challenging and less successful. The adults weighed much more than I did. The "seat" required a much thicker and stronger branch to make it snap-proof. I found out that my hatchet had lost its sharp edge and that made my job of cutting wood much harder. So the second toilet intended for the adults turned out too flimsy. At least I tried.

The days were long and generally uneventful. Some days I felt obligated to spend my time with the Polish girl but not often. Our problem was that we spoke different languages. Most of the time she just sat near me or followed me around when I gathered firewood. When I could, I preferred to sit alone on my tree stump outside in my snow bunker and daydream. This ancient stump seemed a lot like petrified wood, smooth and hard, but yet somehow, warm to the touch. It provided my lookout and my private space.

On sunny days the snowy mountain across from me, rising above the valley, seemed to shine in the sunlight, one brilliant peak among many, a view that brought me a certain kind of peace. At the same time, it beckoned me to know it or climb it, to consider what was on the other side. The other side of that mountain might have even meant freedom, in fact, the very rest of my life. As I pondered my situation, fearful and frightening as it was, it still felt like some kind of grand adventure. Sometimes, while I sat alone, I visualized a world filled with kind and loving people living in beautiful houses with tree-lined promenades. Other times, when frightened by some noise or distant sounds, I returned to thoughts about my escape which I was secretly committed to if the Nazis ever discovered our hideout. I had scoped out several dense trees that I knew I could climb and hide in if the Nazi's ever came back. I would take care of myself.

This much I knew— I had developed a fear of being with adults. I did not trust them, especially since so many showed signs of depression, even hopelessness. I dreamt of a better world and hoped for a better life, and, most importantly, counted on my own strength and confidence to escape and survive.

It became awfully crowded in the shack now that we had taken in Mr. and Mrs. Blech, the wanderers. None of us had the heart to turn them away, to tell them that we had no room or responsibility to give them shelter. For us Orthodox, pious Jews, it was a mitzvah, a blessing, to help save lives. Although we knew next to nothing about them, we felt we must always act like our forefather Abraham and his wife Sara who invited strangers into their tent. In the Bible, they were commanded by *Elohim* [God] to extend utmost hospitality. So, we shared with them the tight space where we slept, the air we breathed, the food we barely had, and our only common possession– the pot-belly stove for central heating and communal kitchen cooking.

Before they came, we had room on the floor for six to sleep comfortably. Now we all had to sleep on our sides, squeezed one against the other. I slept between Anyu and Apu. If I needed to turn from my left side to the right, they had to follow suit. I noticed that Apu and Anyu had been praying more. Apu, who had brought his siddur with him, put on his tefillin and phylactery first thing in the morning, covered his head with his tallis, and read through the entire *shachrit* service, the Jewish morning prayer. My poor Apu. Due to our deficient diet, he had begun complaining often of weakness. It was not surprising, given the large amount of delicious, home-cooked food he was used to consuming when we were living in Prešov. In addition to the ongoing pain in his leg, he had frequent spells of light-headedness.

Amid dwindling supplies and the lack of nourishment, there were some signs of hope and salvation. One night I heard unfamiliar, deep rumbling sounds. It wasn't clear at first which direction they were coming from. I brought it to everyone's attention and asked them to try and identify them. The Polish man thought that they were coming from the direction of Zakopane, a Polish town on the other side of the Tatra Mountains. He thought they sounded like cannons.

"*Dos ist die milchume*," (It must be the war.) he said in Yiddish, "fighting between the Russians and the Germans. Sounds to me like the Germans are retreating from the heavy Russian artillery. They must be crippled at this point. But I hope the Russians get to us soon before we all perish from hunger."

He and my parents often spoke Yiddish to each other. Most Eastern European Jews knew this language. I wished I could understand it so that I could have conversed with him as well. Anyu told me he was a very smart man. Maybe I could have learned some things if only I understood. I did know some German words, similar to Yiddish, but pronounced differently, although not enough for a conversation.

Within a few days, the rumbling noises grew louder. They sounded like they were coming from the opposite side, from the Hron Valley, just below our mountain. One night my curiosity made me descend a ridge downhill from our lean-to. As I peered below, I could not believe my eyes. Amidst the rumbling sounds were fiery balls —cannon balls, flying in the air from east to west and vice-versa. I went to get Anyu and Apu and the others. We stood together on the ridge watching two dueling and desperate armies fire heavy artillery at each other. But it was clear; the Germans were being forced back to the west, retreating into Germany. This dazzling spectacle cheered us all up. We hoped the front would move on toward the west rapidly and end our struggle. We were hugging and kissing one another, expecting to be liberated at any time.

Bedrich 'Frici' Štaub

CHAPTER 38

Apu

Sadly, our celebration was premature. Two weeks passed and we saw no change in the two armies' positions. With each passing day we grew more disappointed, even discouraged. I caught the adults teary-eyed, getting weaker, or some days, just despondent. My dear Apu, my hero, who taught me the "do-re-mi" of music, how to read the notes, who faithfully dragged me to the *kino* to see Walt Disney cartoons and American Westerns, who taught me the first steps of tap dancing, was starting to fall apart emotionally, losing faith. He behaved irrationally. He finally declared that he could no longer cope with the difficult, hopeless situation in these mountains anymore.

"Tomorrow morning I am going to leave," he announced to Anyu and me. "I am going to walk down the mountain to Bobrovček whether you join me or not. I cannot stay here. I am done."

The three of us held a meeting. Anyu and I tried to put some sense into his confused head. "Frici," she said, "you'll be arrested as soon as you enter the village. You will end up in a concentration camp for sure." She looked at me with sad eyes and asked, "Osika, do you want to join Apu? If yes, then I will go too. But what do we gain if we give ourselves up to the Nazis now? Most likely we'll all be killed. I'd rather die of starvation here as a free person. Osika, you decide. But I think it won't be much longer. The Russians might liberate us any day now."

I couldn't believe my mother putting this difficult decision on my shoulders, an unexpected and awful burden. But I knew how I felt. I knew my father was making a grave mistake. "Apu, I'm staying here with Anyu," I said. "I'm going to pray to *Pán Božko* and he will save us." I kept hoping that Apu would change his mind by morning but he was determined to carry out his plan.

"Apu, please don't leave us!" I called out and began to weep as he started to walk away from us the next morning, limping slowly down the hill, his walking stick in one hand. I saw tears in his eyes too as he turned toward us, but then he quickly turned around and headed on down the mountain without another glance. Anyu and I, hand-in-hand, watched him leave and then hugged one another in silence, devastated. We had no words to comfort each other, nothing but tears to cloud our last image of the man we loved. This unexpected and painful parting took place on an overcast and cold winter day, the second week in February, 1945. When Apu was completely out of sight, I turned and buried my face in Anyu's coat and sobbed, confused, angry and abandoned, my heart broken into pieces.

Ferocious battles between the Germans and the Russians were being fought in the valley below, the endless sound of gunfire echoing off the mountains. We hoped it would lead to something good. Anyu and I entrusted our souls to the Almighty and maintained a firm conviction in our ability to pull through these difficult days. We kept busy doing the simple things we had been doing every day, but with heightened urgency. Anyu combed through my hair, searching for lice that infested all of us, everywhere, including our clothes and entire bodies. Every day we had to delouse ourselves. Then I would search Anyu's hair with a special comb designed for this purpose. We had to kill every single louse. I squeezed them between two fingernails. It was disgusting but it had to be done. The days went by slowly. As hard as I tried not to think about Apu, I could not get him out of my mind. "Why would he choose to leave us behind?" I asked my mother repeatedly, despondent and disappointed.

She answered me tenderly. "Osika, our Apu is a wonderful man and I love him very much. Unfortunately, he is not strong. We have to forgive him for what he is doing. Let's hope he finds some decent, caring person in the village who will hide him and take care of him."

Once more my mother had entrusted my life to her care. It seemed that she was always the responsible one, thinking about our family's survival. I accepted her forgiving explanation. There was nothing else I could do.

Our fellow fugitives looked at us with pitiful eyes, not knowing what to say. They felt sorry for Apu and for my mother and me and tried to console us with comments like, "Don't worry. He'll be careful not to get caught," or "Maybe he'll bring back some food for us." Mr. Blech's comment infuriated me though. "God save us if they catch him. We'll all be endangered."

Something evil lurked about this man called Blech. I could not stand him. I wished he would leave and find some other hiding place.

As one long day faded into evening, I still felt sad about Apu being gone. While finishing my chores and about to enter our lean-to, I heard footsteps. I began to survey our surroundings, looking in all directions. Suddenly, I saw a person wearing a hat, carrying a cane, and walking slowly in our direction. Because it was almost dark, I didn't recognize the image at first. And then, as he came closer, I blurted out, "Apu? Is that you?"

No answer. But soon I could see him clearly, so I called out, "Anyu, Anyu, come quick!" My mother stepped out of the lean-to and of course, recognized him at once, overjoyed.

"Frici, are you OK? Is anyone following you?" She threw her arms around him. He stopped and began to sob loudly. "My dear beloveds, please forgive me my selfishness."

We entered the lean-to and he admitted that he never reached the village. His leg had begun to hurt terribly, so he was forced to turn around. He had to stop and rest several times.

"May God forgive my weakness," he said. "I hope we will all be saved soon. And if not, we will all die here together. May those Nazis and Fascists burn in hell for what they have done!"

All of us cried ourselves to sleep that night. Tears of joy, not pain. We were so happy that he returned safely. Up until then, I had never heard my father, a man of peace, express his feelings in such a hateful way. I think it might just have been another way of showing his helplessness and desperation.

The food situation grew more and more difficult. We still had a few potatoes, some dried salami, and a few dried beans and onions, but at this point, we mostly drank water and ate tiny portions of garlic. Anyu hid a potato and everyday sliced a thin piece, baked it on top of the stove, and made me eat it. I still had enough energy to walk around and do my chores.

"There must be something growing in this forest that's edible," I announced, and went searching further uphill, pulling a branch behind me so I could retrace my steps. Walking further up, my eyes detected a bush with red berries. I rushed over to touch them. I picked one and was reminded, since the time I was very young, that many fruits were poisonous, and I should never put them in my mouth. I hesitated, but then thought, maybe these were not that kind. I tasted one briefly and spit the skin into my hand. Waiting for some sign of poisoning, I was relieved when nothing happened. I put another in my mouth and made a request to God, *please don't poison me,* then bit down on the whole thing, expecting a bitter, killer taste. Surprisingly, it was sour, but I liked sour foods, so that was not a problem. At the same time, I was waiting for the poison to start its attack. After a few minutes of no adverse symptoms, I got excited! Perhaps we could eat these berries! I picked a handful and rushed back to our hiding place. "Anyu, look what I found! These berries grow on a bush not very far from here."

"Be careful, Osika, they are probably poisonous," she warned.

"No, they're not."

"How do you know?"

"I ate one and nothing happened to me!"

The Polish man heard me talking and said, "Give me one, let me see it. Yes, these are edible. They are called *brusince.* We ate them coming over the mountains."

"Good," said Anyu happily, "I can make a soup using these berries." She went to work right away using the bunch I brought with me. The next day I returned to the bush and emptied it of all its fruit. For a few days we lived on berry soup and thrived. Like manna in the desert, it sustained us.

CHAPTER 39

Salvation Comes in Many Forms

One February morning, Anyu woke me up from my sleep. She glanced at the opening and said in her softest voice, "Shhh. Someone is walking around outside." I sat up to check and listened. Sure enough, I heard footsteps in the snow. Everyone else lay sleeping soundly. As many times before, my curiosity made me investigate. I stepped over a couple of people carefully, so that I didn't wake them up, slowly opened the flimsy 'door' to the outside, and realized it was blocked halfway up by snow that had fallen overnight. I started to push harder until, through a narrow gap in the snow, I saw a young man on skis stomping around a few yards away from our lean-to with a puzzled look on his face. He carried a rifle on one shoulder and a pouch hung from the other. He definitely resembled the partisans who used to visit us in the cabins. I got brave, pushed open the door, and stood up to look at him.

"Little boy, what are you doing here in the wilderness? Are you alone or with your parents?" he asked in Slovak, obviously surprised.

I explained to him that we came here to hide from the war down in the Vah Valley.

He took a good look at my skinny body and asked, "Do you have any food?"

"No, not really." At that moment he reached into his pouch and pulled out a large piece of bread. I turned around and shouted, "Anyu, Apu, everybody! Come for bread."

Soon enough, they all crawled out and faced this nice partisan who was on a mission, delivering secret orders to his brothers in another unit a few miles away. We all took part of his wonderful gift, slowly and sparingly. Anyu and the Polish woman gave him a great big hug and thanked him for sharing his food with us. The Polish man walked over, reached into his pocket and showed him a pretty diamond ring, saying, "If you bring us more food, some meat or anything that will help keep us alive until we are liberated, we'll give you this ring. It's worth a lot of money."

The partisan smiled at the Polish man and said, "Here in the mountains such a ring is worth nothing to me, but, nevertheless, if I am able to find more food, I will try. These days, with thousands of Nazi thugs roaming around our villages and the fighting going on in the valley, even we have difficulty with food supplies."

He ended with, "May God help you." We all cried after he left, thanking the Almighty for this miracle. A small piece of bread meant a lot to us. He also cheered us up with his comment that very soon the Russians would mount a major offensive to drive the German army out of the Vah Valley once and for all. "And when that happens," he said, "everyone will be able to return home."

Several days later I was sitting on my tree stump behind my bunker of snow admiring the beauty of the sunlit, surrounding nature when my eyes focused on a black dot moving downhill on the opposite, snow-covered mountain. As I had seen these moving dots before I didn't get too excited because they were usually hunters returning to the mountain road that led to one of the villages and back to their homes. When I glanced back at the mountainside again however, I noticed that this person had crossed the road and was walking down to the small valley between the two mountains instead of turning and continuing on the road.

This required more careful surveillance on my part. I figured there was no need to panic because whoever it was might get on the path running in a parallel direction to the road. Unfortunately, I couldn't see all the way down to the bottom of our mountain from my viewpoint, so I sat and waited to see what would happen next.

About fifteen minutes later, I discerned a bounding black dot moving in my direction. I realized this was the head of a person wearing a fur hat like the ones our partisans wore. I raced back and shared this information with the adults who were awake. Then I returned to my post and continued to track the traveler's movement. The next thing I noticed was something like a large rock or package carried on his shoulder. The closer he got, the clearer it became that, indeed he was heading toward us. And then, almost instantly, I recognized him— the partisan who gave us the chunk of bread. I hurried back to the shack again and made a loud announcement that the bread man was returning. The whole group crawled out and lined up to welcome him.

He approached with a big smile on his face and a large piece of raw beef on his shoulder. "This is all I could get for you. The meat should restore your energy. Eat it sparingly. And yes, my partisan brothers and I have decided that if the front does not move westward in a week or so, we are going to cut through the foothills along the Vah Valley to the Russian side. They need us. It is time. If you want, you can come with us."

"Really?" said Apu, smiling for the first time in days. "How long a trip is it?"

"If the weather is good, one day. But if there is a storm, we will have to either bed down for the night wherever we are or continue walking in the dark. You don't have to tell me now."

At that moment the Polish man pulled out the diamond ring again from his pocket, handed it to the partisan, gave him a big hug, and said, "We are going with you whenever you pick us up." Then he added, "Whoever doesn't want to go with the partisans can stay here," looking straight at us. I didn't understand why but knew for certain that I trusted the partisan's decision. We would join him.

Now that we had some sustenance, we also had renewed hope. The mood changed for the better. A guessing game started among the adults. One person suggested, "They'll probably choose a snowy day with less visibility to depart, so if the enemy patrols spot us, it'll be easier to avoid them." Many other theories of how and when we would leave floated around the lean-to.

My main concern was Apu. Would he be able to keep up with the group during its mostly downhill hike? I was really excited about the prospect of joining the partisans on their march toward liberation. Before falling asleep in the evenings, I always prayed to be awakened early in the morning and told to dress quickly with the words, "We are leaving!" I never gave up hope.

Many evenings and mornings came and went since the partisan came with the meat. In the meantime, a critical thing happened. One night, I was startled in my sleep by a person stepping over my legs on his or her way out. In the dark, I could not figure out who it was, but when the door to the outside opened, the silhouette of Mr. Blech appeared. I figured he needed to relieve himself. A while later he returned and went back to sleep. A couple nights later the same thing happened. For some reason I became suspicious of his nightly outings. The last time he was outside in the freezing cold for much longer than it takes to go to the toilet. I made up my mind to investigate his peculiar behavior. The opportunity finally presented itself.

As soon as the door closed behind him, I quickly but silently put on my shoes and warm jacket and tiptoed to the door. I opened it a crack and peeked out. There he was, standing by a tree, looking upward, this way and that. Then he started to climb the tree. When his back was to me, I snuck out the door, walked cautiously to the tree he was climbing, and stopped behind a bush to observe. It dawned on me that the tree he was on was the same one where the Polish man hung our beef. The meat, wrapped in a heavy cloth, hung halfway up the tree to protect it from roaming animals and keep it frozen so it would not spoil. He was reaching up with his hands and a pocket-knife. I understood! He was slicing off a piece of meat. "Bastard!"I wanted to scream at him. *Not now*, I stopped myself, *I don't want to wake up everyone.*

"*Sviňa!*" (Swine!) I kept repeating to myself as I snuck back into the shack, lay down, and pretended to sleep. A few minutes later, the thief snuck back to his spot and lay down too, feigning sleep. But not exactly. I heard some whispering between him and his wife; he was sharing the spoils with her. They were both guilty of stealing from the rest of us. As I was very agitated, I stayed awake almost all night.

I hated them.

In the morning, I woke up and waited for Anyu to rise so I could tell her what I saw the night before. And of course, right after I described to her what went on with Blech, she walked outside with Apu and the Polish man to confront the thief. Within minutes, a noisy argument ensued that involved everybody. Apu and the Polish man became so angry that for a few seconds, I thought they were going to kill Blech. He and his wife were told to get out.

"You pretend to be such dignified people, but you are trash," said Anyu.

Mrs. Blech started to cry and begged us to allow them to stay. "Please don't make us leave. We will freeze to death if you throw us out. I promise you; my husband won't do it again. We love all of you. Hunger drove him to this ugly act. Please give us another chance, we swear it won't happen again."

Of course, no one had the vicious intention to banish them, or throw them to the wolves, as the saying goes. "We are all Jews here, trying to survive, to save our lives from the modern day Amalekites (a people who were Biblical enemies of the Jews long ago). Let us just forgive and forget," said Anyu, attempting to restore peace.

Mr. and Mrs. Blech were allowed to stay but after the incident they were mostly ignored by everyone. Before all this happened, I used to have interesting discussions with the Blechs, but no more. They behaved selfishly, they acted on their own behalf. In my eyes, they were not Jewish. Jews are taught that in order to survive, we have to help each other, not steal from each other. Besides, it is written in the Ten Commandments. "Thou shall not steal."

CHAPTER 40

Now or Never

The mood had changed quite considerably since the meat incident. It felt like we all went into mourning. The adults barely spoke to each other. In the midst of all the initial arguments, Blech admitted to pinching some fat off the meat and eating it raw for energy. I made an error telling Anyu that he was slicing off the meat. I realized I would have to be more accurate in the future, reporting what I observed.

The first of March came and went and not much changed in the valley. We kept hearing the same artillery barrage as before, however, the earth now rumbled day and night. I had to be on alert more than ever because there were so many more airplane flyovers. Some were German and some were Allied forces' bombers flying in groups high above the mountains on their way to destroy the Nazis. I always waved at them, even though I knew they couldn't see me from so high up in the sky. It just gave me a good feeling. It made me believe that the world was finally rising up to a terrible evil.

On the morning of March 3rd, 1945, in the dark of pre-dawn, we were startled by a loud, familiar voice. It was our partisan. "Friends, this is it! We are on our way down. Those joining us have five minutes to assemble. We will leave without you if you are not ready. Take only essentials."

We rushed about. No one wished to be left behind. Silent chaos, pushing, shoving, and a dilemma – what to take, what to leave, even though we had so little.

"Let's move it; only a couple minutes left," he urged.

We crawled out of the lean-to, one-by-one, startled, excited, and scared, all at the same time.

"Single-file line please, no talking. If you must stop for any reason, you'll have to catch up quickly. We can't be responsible for any of you. Now, follow me!"

I could hardly believe it. We were leaving at last. The partisan led us downhill a couple hundred yards where we joined a group of five others armed with automatic weapons and hand-grenades. They led, we followed, with our partisan friend at the tail. The pace was steady; not too fast, not too slow. Every so often the procession stopped. One of the partisans was sent forward as a scout while we waited. These stops were helpful for Apu since he could lean on his cane and take the pressure off his leg. If the wait was long, we had a chance to sit and rest. I wanted to be closer to the partisans but Anyu would not let me leave her side. I was the third one from the very end of the line.

We took our orders from our partisan, the one who had befriended us. During the longer stops, he advanced to talk to his buddies. They mapped out a route to follow, but it was not without danger. Chances were high that we might be spotted by a German patrol or by deserters hiding in the mountains. The partisans' goal was to reach the Russian forces as quickly as possible without any armed confrontation with the enemy. If so, and danger came our way, hopefully, they were well-armed enough to protect us all.

At noon, we stopped for a few minutes for a bite and to relieve ourselves. My poor Apu was struggling, in constant pain. Anyu made arrangements with our Polish friend to help hold him up — Anyu on the left, him on the right. Otherwise, thus far the journey had been smooth. But with every passing hour, the fighting in the valley grew louder, especially as we walked closer to the battlefield below. We had roughly four hours until nightfall. The partisans increased the pace since walking in the dark would slow us down considerably.

In the early afternoon, we reached the edge of a large clearing that appeared to be an abandoned German field camp. Hundreds of cases of ammunition, weapons, tents, tables with canteens and unfinished meals, a field kitchen, and a variety of unidentifiable instruments, lay strewn about. I was ecstatic. All this stuff was here for the taking and I couldn't get my hands on any of it. Anyu saw to that. It was the dream of every kid to salvage the spoils of war and I was no different. If only I could have run over and taken a shiny bayonet, a couple of grenades, maybe a pistol. Wow, wouldn't that have been fun? Once we got back to Prešov, I would have shown them off to all my friends.

Anyu grabbed my hand and held it tight, knowing quite well what was going on in my head. We soon found ourselves walking within the boundaries of yesterday's battlefields, hidden, but near an area of live engagement. We were facing a new danger – namely, stray artillery and mortar shells flying overhead. When the shrill scream of one came in our direction, not knowing when or where it might explode, we hit the ground and held our breath. We all praised God when we stood up, unhurt. Even though the German artillery was a short distance to the west of us, our lives were in jeopardy due to occasional errors in firing weapons. The frequency of the explosions diminished the further east we went.

As we walked, I caught a glimpse of the Vah river to the south and, if I strained my eyes, saw strange objects floating in the water. This upset me. Bloated and lifeless, those objects were dead animals, cows, horses, dogs, all victims of warfare. A couple of times Anyu told me not to look. She shielded my view with her body. She said it was disgustingly horrible and didn't want me to see. I did as I was told and turned my head the other way. I could only imagine a human body floating down the river, too. Just as well I didn't look. It was bad enough to see the animals, innocent victims of war.

Before long, daylight slipped into darkness. With less visibility, the partisans changed course and we were once again walking in a forest, at a somewhat slower pace. The snowpack was minimal on the lower elevations. By now we were exhausted, tense, and hoping to reach our destination without any further setbacks. The word from the leader of our pack was that we were about two hours away from the Russian-occupied area, and safety. Slowly the sounds of battle faded behind us.

We were heading toward Žiar, one of the larger villages at the foot of the Tatra Mountains. As total darkness enveloped the forest, with it came an eerie silence. All I could hear were our footsteps tapping on the soft forest floor. We were walking with precision, almost in unison. By this time, we were all numb. The entire experience seemed unreal; I felt like I was in a waking dream with the long-awaited reality of freedom nearly within reach. As we drew closer to our destination, my heart swelled with happiness and my eyes filled with tears. We were so close. We had survived. We would really be free. Yet, in spite of all the signs behind us of an apparent Nazi defeat, for some unexplainable reason, I was also terribly afraid we might not yet reach our goal.

Slovak 18th Anti-Aircraft Artillery Battery
that took part in the Slovak National Uprising, autumn 1944.
Photo: public domain

CHAPTER 41

Liberation At Last

From out of nowhere we heard sharp shouts, gruff voices of men screaming, "*Postoy, Postoy!,*" so loud they almost sounded like gunshots coming from behind the trees. More male voices echoed in the darkness, aiming flashlights and automatic weapons at us. *What now? Were we under arrest?*

Desperate cries of fear came from the adults in our group, but not from the partisans in the lead. They recognized the command "*Postoy!*" In Russian it meant "Stop!" Our reaction changed from shock to exhilaration. The message relayed down from the front of the line. We were now the wards of a Russian patrol and had reached the liberated territory at last!

The Russian soldiers demanded that we obey their orders. We formed a line facing them. The partisans were told to lay down their weapons and submitted to being searched. Next, we were told to raise our arms. One of the soldiers walked by and ordered us in Russian to *davai chasi* (remove our watches). We were all searched, then

237

told politely to follow them in an orderly fashion. This, after they robbed us! But who dared even say a word?

We walked in silence, following them for about half an hour until we entered a poorly lit village. We had arrived in Žiar, our destination. An officer took charge and the partisans left. We were taken to a mess hall, told to wash up, and sit down on wooden benches alongside a big wooden table. Out came a woman with a large pot of soup— steaming hot, potato soup. People were smiling. Some were crying. We were being fed and sheltered. This was the moment when we realized we had truly been liberated.

Anyu, Apu and I fell into each other's arms, hugging and kissing, celebrating our arrival. We were speaking in normal voices to each other for the first time in weeks, our humanity returned. All around the table, everyone ate with enormous appetite, except me.

Anyu looked at me and said, *"Miert nem eszel?"* in Hungarian. (Why aren't you eating?)

"Because I hate potato soup," I answered.

"Ty si sa zbláznil?" (Have you lost your mind?) she asked in Slovak.

She could not convince me. I simply could not stand the smell or taste of potato soup. For some reason, I was not even that hungry. The whole episode had been overwhelming. I kept feeling like the events of the past twenty-four hours were merely a nightmare that I had now awakened from. I had been praying for this moment since we left Prešov and now, my mind was in a state of confusion, or perhaps a state of numbness. I was weak, exhausted and just wanted to sleep. And fortunately, our hosts knew how tired we must have been. Following the meal, the Russians took us to a room with military cots and blankets and I fell asleep immediately.

The next day, our first day of freedom, held a couple of surprises for Anyu and Apu. First, we were told we would have to be patient about returning to Prešov due to the fact that public transportation did not exist. Our return trip would have to be in stages as space became available on departing military vehicles. In short, we were stuck at the mercy of the combined Russian and Czechoslovak Legion's regional temporary headquarters.

Still, the sun was shining and the weather was mild. At this point, we had food and shelter and a real sense of hope, simple things that had been out of reach. We walked through the town observing everything and everybody. Spirits were high. Suddenly, a tall officer walked past us. Anyu stopped, turned around, and called out "Laci!"

He looked at her, hesitated, and then recognized her. "Irénke!" he smiled, and they embraced happily. Apu and I were introduced to this handsome, young officer, formerly a teenage friend from Anyu's hometown, Sobrance. For the next ten minutes or so, she and Laci walked arm-in-arm, having a spirited discussion as Apu and I followed behind. Laci then took charge of our life. First, he handed Anyu a roll of Slovak currency. Second, he transferred us to a house with comfortable beds, and third, booked us on a military truck for the next day that would take us to Poprad, the city where Anyu spent a few days in the hospital on our way to Mikuláš.

The rest of the day we spent meeting and chatting with a few more Jewish soldiers who knew Anyu's and Apu's families. For me, the best experience had been using an indoor toilet and washing with good smelling soap. The next morning we said goodbye to our friends and fellow survivors who were staying behind. We took our meager belongings, including a couple of new pieces of clothing we received upon arrival, and climbed onto the back of the truck. Laci seated Anyu in the cab next to the driver. He kissed her goodbye on the cheek and ordered the driver to proceed.

In addition to our family, the truck bed was filled with a few military men. After a series of stops on the way, dropping off and taking on soldiers, we arrived in Poprad. The driver let us off in front of a private house. The front door was unlocked, so we entered and called out, "Halo, is anyone here?"

The house looked abandoned. The kitchen table had several plates of unfinished food on them. The closet was messy, partially emptied. All signs indicated a hasty departure by members of a family that once occupied this house. At first, we felt uncomfortable, but then my parents said, "Let us not feel sorry for using their home. Most likely they had to escape from here with the Nazi military to escape punishment by the new Czechoslovak regime."

We cleaned up the place and put clean sheets on the beds. Anyu cooked dinner using ingredients we found in the kitchen. It was ironic that this house was walking distance to the municipal hospital Anyu stayed in. The next day we set out on foot to purchase food supplies and inquire about transportation back home. We found out about the next bus departure. "You will have to wait a few days," we were told, due to a shortage of buses. The next morning my parents hired a private taxi. We needed to get home. Soon we were off to the city of my birth– Prešov!

The road was bumpy and crowded with vehicles of all types, some motorized, others pulled by horses or oxen. Traffic moved slowly and we became anxious. The driver was frustrated, especially when cattle or sheep were crossing the road and traffic came to a halt. Occasionally, we saw destroyed military vehicles on either side of the road and beyond. All three of us were uneasy, not knowing what to expect once we got to Prešov.

Upon arrival, with the most minimal resources, we moved into a sparsely furnished second-story apartment. Our former apartment had been occupied by another family and all our belongings taken. Anyu and Apu set about contacting former acquaintances hoping to find information about survivors. It seemed that we were among the very first returnees and it would take some time to get a clearer picture of what happened to family and friends who were sent to concentration camps.

These were difficult times indeed. On one hand, we felt extremely fortunate to have stayed alive and regained our freedom; on the other hand, the tragedy of the Jewish people weighed heavily on our shoulders and in our hearts As Apu slowly absorbed the heartbreaking situation in Prešov and elsewhere, he began searching for his family, and Anyu, for hers. I also inquired about my cousins and close friends. We learned after just a few days in Prešov that approximately 240 Jews thus far had returned to our city out of its original population of 4500 Jewish souls. The numbers were devastating. Just as important was any news about friends and family in Kassa. We were desperate to learn who had survived.

In the aftermath of the war's end, Prešov had become a lawless place, almost uninhabitable. We were advised to proceed cautiously with legal matters as the court system was in disarray, along with the municipality services such as police, health services, transportation, and more. A great deal of prejudice toward returning Jews was blatantly expressed in the streets. We heard unkind comments from Christians resentful of our return to our hometown. People shouted insults like "What? Hitler didn't finish the job?" or "Why did you come back?" I was called a stinking little Jew by kids passing me in the streets. It hurt deeply and made me angry. Coming home was a terrible disappointment.

To think that only some seventy-two hours earlier, I had been hungry and cold, sitting in my bunker, awaiting the moment of liberation, and hopeful of returning to a society that celebrated freedom and condemned bigotry and discrimination. Apparently, some people in Prešov still believed that the regime of hatred and persecution had not been vanquished. The propaganda of Fascist supremacy had found its way deep into their blood. They still hated us and although the dark days of plunder and the theft of Jewish properties were short-lived and the Hlinka Guardists ran off with the retreating Nazi army, some of these para-military thugs and their Fascist supporters yet remained. They continued to shoot off their ugly mouths, causing more pain to the returning survivors whose relatives and friends had perished in the Nazi death camps.

It became clear over time that, although we had come out of hiding and were no longer subject to arrest and deportation, mentally and emotionally we still felt enslaved. Teenage gangs roamed the city harassing people with verbal insults. Almost daily, we heard reports of beatings and shootings and random attacks on civilians. Gang wars took place, dangerous and threatening, due to the use of weapons and live ammunition. Within a few days of our return, I found out that a gang of young Jewish boys was recruiting more members. This was welcome news for me. At this point, I was already ten years old and wished I could join them.

Since our return, I had been bored and restless, hanging around our apartment while my parents were trying to re-establish their business in another storefront. They had been luckier than many other returnees due to their loyal, caring Christian friends, Judge

Šolc and his sister Maria, who continued to operate our store while we were in hiding. They were still there and glad to see us alive. Very few Jewish businesses had been returned to their original owners, mainly because most of the deported businessmen never returned.

Prešov, Slovakia
Photo: postcard-public domain

My grandmother Hermina Grünfeld (center) with her daughters
Rözsi Birnbaum and Sarlota 'Irene' Staub (my mother).
By the end of the war, my grandmother and Aunt Rözsi were murdered, c. 1935

CHAPTER 42

Out of the Ashes

I t was difficult to comprehend the entirety of the loss of Jewish lives all across Europe. German records confirmed that at least one-and-a-half million innocent children under the age of fifteen were exterminated in the Shoah, the Hebrew word for the Holocaust, meaning brutally murdered by being shot, gassed, starved or otherwise brought to their death. Further, we confirmed that the Germans, although losing the war by 1944, had entered Hungary on March 19,1944, and in less than two months, rounded up some 440,000 Jews, victims of the second largest Jewish community in Europe, who were hastily deported from Hungary in 145 trains, mostly headed to Auschwitz-Birkenau in Poland.

Over time, we found out which of our dear relatives had perished in Auschwitz and elsewhere. The list was staggering and left us feeling deeply saddened and emotionally shattered. It pains me even now to list their names. It included Apu's parents, my beloved grandparents Štaub; Anyu's mother, my grandmother Omama Hermina

Grünfeld; my uncles Soli and Pinchas Grünfeld, their wives and four children; Uncle Adolf Grünfeld's wife and their two children; my Aunt Rozsi Birnbaum (Grünfeld) with her husband Armin and their two children Osi and Agi; my Aunt Malcsi (Grünfeld), Anyu's older sister and her daughter Jolánka; my Aunt Rozsi' Štaub's husband Willy Jung; my great-grandmother Maria Degner and her sister Linka; and my two sweet cousins, Irena and Agi Grünfeld who were caught crossing the border between Hungary and Slovakia. The loss was immeasurable, impossible to fathom. Further, without a proper grave site to remember them by, our grief was overwhelming. We prayed that their memories never be forgotten.

My personal list was also long. I lost all my close, early-childhood friends except Eva Nagy, my first school friend in Slovakia. Her parents and grandparents were shot to death by Nazi soldiers during the Slovak uprising. Her escape was miraculous. My dance and singing partner Nadja Majtin from Kassa, Hungary, was deported, along with her parents to Auschwitz in the summer of 1944 where she perished with her family. About twenty-five individuals whom I knew personally did not survive.

None of this made any sense. Those who perished were all wonderful people who didn't deserve to die. Now they were gone, as if they had never existed at all. In addition, I had a sad, lingering feeling that I had lost something else very precious to me—my own childhood. I returned to Prešov feeling old before my time. Never again would I wonder with wide, innocent eyes at the world unfolding around me. I had seen too much.

When I stayed with our relatives, the Zinger family in Kassa (who miraculously survived Auschwitz), I remembered missing my parents terribly and how, on many nights, I cried under the covers before falling asleep. Now, I cried endless tears for my cousins, aunts, uncles, grandparents and wonderful friends who had been taken from this earth. Often, in my prayers, I questioned God, asking why I survived, and they did not. Especially, I missed my cousins Irenka and Agi who were almost like sisters to me. I had felt so very close to them.

Besides my great sadness, I also harbored a great deal of hostility against the Slovak Fascists, the despicable Jew haters, who persecuted us, rounded up our people, and handed them over to the Nazis for slaughter. Following this admission, I tried not to let my anger own me. I knew there had to be a brighter future ahead and it was up to me to make it my own. I had to reclaim my life.

In retrospect, all I can say today is that I am more than grateful that there were decent people in this world who stood by us and remained our friends until the very end. They lived what they believed, accepting and respecting others, even if those people were different than themselves. It goes without saying that this is the way it should always be. It was with great comfort that I could confirm the friendship and loyalty of the Šolc family and go to sleep at night knowing that the entire world had not betrayed us.

The larger lessons learned from my survival of this horrific period have stayed with me for a lifetime, some eighty-five years and counting. Over and over, I have been reminded to never abandon hope, to believe in yourself, and to always look for the good in people.

As I grew into adulthood and our family emigrated to Israel and South America and eventually, to the United States, I took my love of country, my Slavic and Jewish identity, my great love of music and my faith in God wherever I went. All of these things shaped me as a man. I became a dedicated musician and performance artist who sang in many languages, a celebrated songwriter and accordion player, a Jewish community administrator, and more. As a father of a loving family of four (now adult) children, a grandfather of seven grandchildren, and a great-grandfather of two, I want this story to be told to as many generations as possible. Its lessons are universal and timeless, and I am forthright in stating them here. Stand up for what you believe in, protect the rights of others, and treat others as you wish to be treated yourself. Few people today can appreciate the price some of us have paid to live in freedom. I, for one, will never forget it.

I find it essential to mention that in September of 2021, the country of Slovakia made a formal apology about their WWII-era, anti-Jewish laws that stripped Jews of their rights 80 years ago, and for their role in the destruction of its Jewish population. As you now know, Slovakia became a Nazi puppet state and deported its Jews to Nazi death camps, resulting in some 68,000-71,000 Slovak Jews murdered in the Holocaust. Their regret today comes too late for all of those who are gone. But at least, their declaration is an important step toward making amends for its wartime crimes and begins to honor the memory of those who suffered so greatly. For today's new Slovak generation, it might help create a better path into the future.

All I can hope for now is that such a lack of respect for humanity never be seen again, not in your lifetime, or ever. Toward that goal, I ask you to please share my story with your friends and family so we can all create a better world.

**POVERENÍCTVO
SLOVENSKEJ NÁRODNEJ RADY**
PRE VECI VNÚTORNÉ,expozitúra v Košiciach

Číslo: 3.198/IV-1945.   Košice,dňa 16.mája 1945.

Predmet:Staub Bedrich,Prešov,zmena
priezviska.

V ý m e r .

Na základe §-u 8 zákona číslo 31/1945 Sl.zák.vy-
hovujem žiadosti Bedricha Štauba,narodeného dňa 20.augusta 1902 v
Košiciach,príslušného do Prešova a povoľujem zmenu jeho priezviska
na " S l á d e k ".

Táto zmena vzťahuje sa aj na jeho manzelku Irenu rod.
Grünfeldovú,narodenú dňa 10.mája 1914 v Sobranciach a na maloleté detí:
Oskára Stauba,narodeného dňa 19.marca 1935 v Prešove.

O tom sa upovedomuje:

1./ Bedrich Staub v Prešove s tým,aby jeden exemplár tohoto výmeru
predložil so žiadostou príslušným štátnym matričným úradom cielom opra-
venia matričných záznamov.

Zástupca povereníka:

Legal document officially changing our family surname from Štaub to Sladek.

Kosice, Slovakia (formerly Kassa, Hungary)
Oskar Sladek and Sarlota 'Irene' Sladek, c. 1946

CHAPTER 43

1945-1949

My journey as presented in the previous pages does not end with our return to the town of Prešov. No, the Holocaust did not end for me until my feet touched down upon the soil of Israel, the only place where a Jew could live in freedom. In brief, the following summary covers the time from our salvation by the Russians to the next momentous chapter of our life in the miraculous, newly founded country, the home of the Jewish people.

Following our resettlement in Prešov, I joined a local Jewish youth group training to mount a Jewish defense war against those Christians who taunted us. We had managed to collect assorted weapons including pistols, grenades, sling shots, bayonets and more. All of this I kept secret from my parents, of course. For me, it was a way to try and control my pent-up anger and frustration. After many confrontations, internments in jail of some of our members, and even a few fatalities between our gang and our antisemitic enemies, those who hated Jews, the city government cracked down on the gang wars and brought them to a halt. By the fall of 1945, the city council, with the help of the police force, broke up and disbanded the gangs, just in time for the gang members to start a new school year with new rules and a brand-new curriculum.

The sad reality of our homecoming was deepened by the fact that a mere 284 Jews returned from the camps, or were hiding, to a city that did not want them. Many of its citizens were compliant in the roundups by simply doing nothing and turning a blind eye. They pretended they didn't know what was going on. Their hypocrisy was too much for our family to bear.

My parents decided to move away from Prešov to nearby Košice (Kassa), the largest city in eastern Slovakia. In Košice, they planned to open a new store like the one we had in Prešov. It is more than painful for me to think that the very first store, started by my grandparents so many years ago, was completely Aryanized—taken over and made into a Christian-owned business, with no regard for my grandfather Štaub, who, along with his wife, died in Auschwitz and had no way of being honored or remembered.

Once we moved, my parents rented a nice apartment and opened up shop on the newly-renamed street *Masarykova ulica* (which from 1938 until 1945 was *Hlinkova ulica*). This apartment was located a few blocks away from their new store. It didn't take long for the business to thrive. Many happy customers became our best advertisers. By then, we had changed our surname so it didn't sound German in origin anymore. I was now Osi Sladek. Soon, the reputation of the store spread throughout the region. People traveled from far away to shop at "Sladek's."

Apu expanded the merchandise to offer the latest records and record players. Anyu introduced an imported line of luxurious baby carriages. My Uncle Jeno from Trebisov (Anyu's older brother) and his wife Terez moved to Košice and became partners in the business. I even pitched in, assembling baby carriages since I enjoyed working with my hands. I did such a good job that I received a weekly allowance and for the first time in my life had money in my pocket. I soon befriended the owner of a tobacco store that sold stamps from all over the world and got hooked on collecting postage stamps. I used my own money and bought my first set issued by some remote island nation. I visited the shop at least twice a week and within a year, filled up a large, thick album with thousands of stamps, spending all my allowance on my hobby.

In Košice, we moved into a villa, an elegant house, owned by retired Judge Koncser who lived there with his wife. Surviving relatives, my aunt Rûzena, (Apu's sister who survived the war with her baby Turko) and my Uncle Tidi moved in with us as well.

The villa was located on a quiet street behind the largest park in Košice, not far from the train station. Uncle Jeno and Aunt Terez moved into a second-floor apartment nearby in order to be close. I liked living there. Since moving to Košice, my parents showered me with a number of amazing gifts including an air rifle and an air pistol. I was determined to eliminate the invasion of mice from our veranda where many foodstuffs were stored. Outdoors, I performed target practice on wild birds. Secretly, I spent many hours creating nasty pranks in the park and also practicing them upon suspecting pedestrians from my Aunt's second-story window. I knew it was wrong, but I did it anyway. Perhaps it was my way of taking personal revenge on adults in general.

Oskar with cousin Rozsi Zinger
in front of Judge Koncser's villa in Kosice,
after the Zinger family miraculously returned from Auschwitz, 1945

My life was busy with tutored piano lessons, English language lessons, and preparation for my bar mitzvah which took place in March of 1948. I also attended Hebrew school to learn how to read Hebrew. The teacher was very strict and used a stick to keep our group of twelve-year-old boys in line. In addition, I took private lessons from the *melamed* (teacher) to learn my *parsha* (portion from the Torah) in time for my bar mitzvah date. I further had to learn the Ashkenazi pronunciation of Hebrew and Yiddish words.

The day of reckoning arrived. The service was scheduled in a chapel adjacent to a dining room where guests could enjoy a kosher meal following the religious service. This arrangement was due to the desecrated condition of the Jewish synagogues in Košice. A few days after our arrival there, I happened to walk past the beautiful synagogue on Frangepan Street where I sang in the choir at the age of eight. I was shocked by the sight of Hungarian cavalry and their horses occupying the interior of this sacred Jewish house of prayer. Staring at the soldiers, I wanted to scold them. They saw me and shouted, "Move on you little Jew" – what are you staring at?" I trembled in fear. Theses soldiers may have lost the war but not the hatred they harbored for our people. I walked away defeated, wishing I had the strength of Samson to smite them and teach them a lesson.

My Bar Mitzvah day arrived. As I readied myself to go up to the Torah to read my portion, I looked around, surrounded by a roomful of valiant human beings holding back their tears, most wishing that their loved ones would somehow miraculously reappear from oblivion. Many in the room had lost children, spouses, parents, and siblings. As I looked at my Uncle Jeno and Aunt Terez, guilt washed over me. I wanted to know their thoughts as they watched me about to fulfill the mitzvah of entering adulthood, becoming a full-fledged member of the Jewish community. I stumbled through the ceremony, but with the help of my *melamed* (teacher), I pushed ahead over my mistakes until I finished, evoking tears throughout the room. Perhaps they were tears of joy? Doubtful. How could any of us celebrate without our cousins, grandparents, aunts, uncles, and friends by our side?

OSCAR SLADEK

My Bar Mitzvah photo with my parents.
Kosice, March 13, 1948

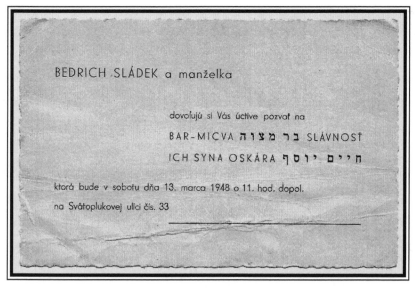

Bedrich Sladek and spouse cordially invite you to the
celebration of their son's Bar Mitzvah Saturday March 13, 1948 at 11:00am

Anyu and Apu congratulated, kissed and hugged me and we all cried together. This event in my life, which over many decades I had almost forgotten until I began to write this book, was a bittersweet celebration for the survivors. My dear parents bought me many fine gifts, but the best of all, was the news that Anyu was pregnant. I would finally have a sibling, the first joyful news in our family in a very long time. In the meantime, Aunt Ružena found a new husband, Nandor Glasel, and gave birth to my new cousin Štefko. The Zingers, who had so lovingly watched over me, returned to reestablish themselves in Košice. Both of my cousins Roszi and Judit got married. Fortunately, all of Anyu's surviving siblings settled down near us.

Every Sabbath we saw our relatives and friends in the synagogue and almost every Sunday they came to our apartment for a musical gathering and refreshments. My Uncle Jeno and Uncle Adolf, the cantor (Jewish clergy who sings the prayers), were the vocalists, along with Judit and Rozsi on the piano. Apu played the violin, and I played the drums. Sometimes a family friend joined in on the clarinet. Anyu and her friends were in charge of dancing the *czardas*, a Hungarian folk dance. I loved Sundays for the music which restored some semblance of joy and happiness in our lives, a never-ending source I would turn to many times over during my long lifetime.

News on the radio was all about the fighting in Palestine. We sat glued to the shortwave model we owned. Members of the new temporary government headed by David Ben Gurion were about to declare independence for a new Jewish state called Israel. My friends and I met every Shabbat afternoon with our *madrich* (counselor) to learn about Zionism. We sang Hebrew songs, danced Jewish folk dances, and emotionally prepared ourselves to one day make *aliya* (to go up) to Israel. We became members of *B'nai Akiva,* a youth movement.

Some of us young survivors who had been in hiding had previously formed an organization to stop intimidation and verbal harassment of Jews in the city of Košice. We met once-a-week to instill courage enough to defend ourselves against those who would hurt us. Members were obligated to report antisemitic incidents to me, that is, actions hostile to Jewish people, then I consulted my assistants, and we decided on the course of action. We confronted hostile kids and even acted on reports of adult antisemitism as well. Then we passed that information to our parents, hoping that they would follow through with the Jewish Community Council. One afternoon, one of our members overheard a small group of women complaining about the return of the lousy Jews to Košice. "We were better off without them." "Too bad Hitler couldn't kill them all." We confronted these women, demanding an apology for their insults. They turned to their husbands who called the police on us. That incident forced us to disband our activities, although we still had our weekly meetings. We were forced by our parents to conduct ourselves in a lawful manner.

In 1946 and 1947 when I was but twelve years of age, a Jewish action-oriented project called *B'richa* (to escape) secretly smuggled Hungarian Holocaust survivors from Hungary to Palestine via Czechoslovakia. Our city of Košice became one of the stopover points for groups of those housed illegally in temporary safe houses. In order to continue their journey to the next stopover, they had to be smuggled from their hiding places across town to the train station. To attract the least amount of exposure and suspicion, the agent in charge selected local Jewish youth to act as guides. I was selected because of my ability to speak their language.

Photo of me on the Kosice Village steps, 1947

From this moment on I held a very big secret. I did it to perform a great *mitzvah* or good deed of *pikuach nefesh,* Hebrew for saving souls. Every time I got the call I had to invent another excuse to leave the villa for an hour or so after dark. Entrusted with a group of four or five people at a time, I was fully aware of the consequences if caught by the local authorities. If necessary, I was empowered to change the route for the sake of the safety of the people I was leading. It was very satisfying to help out these refugees on their way to Palestine, hoping to someday go there as well. At the train station, I handed them over to an agent who helped them board the train to Bratislava near the Austrian border.

Once I made it safely to the station and watched them board the train, it was a great relief. The need for my help came randomly without any warning, sometimes with only half an hour advance notice. When my parents ultimately found out about my involvement, they warned me to be extremely cautious. They worried about my getting in trouble with the law. But they understood, because while I was staying with Anyu's sister's family in Kosice, they once gave temporary refuge to fugitive Polish Jews. I felt it was my duty to help survivors.

Heated debates regarding independence for a Jewish state continued in the United Nations, although Arab countries were strongly opposed. The U.N. voted for a partition plan, which would create two independent nations side-by-side, one Jewish, one Palestinian. Meanwhile, thousands of Holocaust survivors were being smuggled into Palestine on ships, breaking the British blockade. Fighting between the Jewish *Haganah* (military forces) and Arab armies resulted in many casualties on both sides.

Two months after I turned thirteen, on May 14, 1948, the world waited for an important announcement from Tel-Aviv. The familiar voice on our radio of David Ben Gurion (who became the first prime minister of this new nation) narrated a proclamation on behalf of the Jewish Agency establishing a free homeland for the Jewish people called Israel. We were ecstatic, hugging and kissing one another with joy! No one could have dreamed that after such a lengthy period of persecution by the Christian civilized world would we be so quickly granted a homeland of our own so soon.

Following this announcement, some people said Israel was created out of guilt. Others were more cynical, saying that since the Nazis failed to annihilate us completely, many Christians hoped that the remnant would leave for Israel and thus, Europe would be free of Jews. From that day on, I was inspired by the idea of the *chalutzim* (Hebrew for *the pioneers*), and helped with the task of building a new Jewish democratic country. No such thing had existed in 2000 years. I told my parents about my decision to immigrate to Israel, a sacred opportunity not to be missed. To me, Israel was nothing short of a miracle, a gift from the Almighty.

Our youth group meetings took on new meaning. We were excited about leaving the hateful society that betrayed us. We studied the Hebrew language, discussed the progress of the war, and the opportunities available when we reached the land of our dreams. Immigration rules stated parental permission was needed to apply for immigration, but not past the age of 16.

The Jews of Košice were split on the issue of immigration, especially since our government had become Communist. Recent elections turned our lives upside down. The economy had been socialized and businesses taken away by the state. No more private ownership of stores. Incredible as it seemed, Anyu and Apu began working in their own store as state employees, a repeat of what had happened in Prešov. Politics of the new ĈSR – *Ĉesko Slovenska Republika* (under the political command of the Soviet Union, liberators of Eastern Europe who beat back the German forces) changed drastically with frequent arrests, purges and political trials. Citizens were urged to join the Communist party which promised better opportunities and a safer future. Young people were organized into work brigades and school curriculums emphasized socialist theories and the study of Russian language and literature.

I had to adapt, and I did. I actually enjoyed learning Russian, just as I agreed with the appealing concept of equality, as I understood it. With religious activities curtailed, I looked forward to the weekend outings with my school friends. We were assigned to work details like road cleaning projects and beautification of parks and other public facilities. I liked wearing my special shirt with the red kerchief around my neck. In school we sang the national anthems of our country and Russia. Emphasis was also on physical fitness, gymnastics and track meets.

Just as I enjoyed Hungarian musicals during my year in Kassa, I now loved going to concerts of Russian army choirs and performances by colorful dance groups. I was moved by the energy of the dancers and the beautiful melodies of the singers, most of which stayed with me for years, eventually to be preserved on my musical recordings, compilations of the many folksongs I learned over time in Czech, Slovak, Yiddish, Russian, Hebrew and English. These were the cultural seeds planted in my soul that gave birth to my later career as a composer, song writer and singer.

During this time, my family did not join the Communist party. As a matter of fact, very few Jews became party members. It didn't make our lives any better or easier. A form of discrimination against non-members surfaced however, causing concern to my parents regarding our future.

Most of our friends were preparing to emigrate to Israel by the summer of 1949. Meanwhile, Anyu was carrying a baby to be born in August. Life was filled with excitement. That summer I improved my tennis skills and continued my piano lessons. My teacher pushed classical pieces while I preferred learning more jazz-oriented music. My English language lessons were progressing well. But day and night, my mind was occupied with the thoughts of making my way to the land of my forefathers; to become a pioneer, to fight for the Jewish peoples' freedom. I became obsessed with the idea of Israel.

On August 5th, Anyu gave birth to my sister, Miriam (Maria) named after my Štaub great-grandmother. I was not alone anymore. I got to hold her in my arms and calm her down when she cried. It was good to have a new baby in the family. The focus was on her and no longer on me. She brought us all a sense of hope for the future.

With my baby sister, Miriam "Mimi", 1948

With the many tragedies and losses in our family, the Grünfelds remained faithful to Judaism and to Orthodoxy. Apu's brothers on the other hand, had lost faith in our religion and, as the war ended, married non-Jewish spouses. Many survivors we knew questioned the existence of God and denounced their religion. Apu's sister Ružena married a Jewish man, Nandor, who had lost his wife and child in the Holocaust, and moved to make their home in Žilina in western Slovakia. They had a son, Stefko. Nandor Glasel, an avid Zionist, took his new family to Israel in the spring of 1949. They settled in the German colony in the city of Haifa.

I still enjoyed living in Košice which had approximately 70,000 citizens. Before the war there were around 15,000 Jews. Now, we had been reduced to a mere 4000. The city had a modern streetcar running the length of the main street which I rode to school. Shortly after the war ended, the Joint Distribution Committee (created to help Jewish survivors) opened an office and warehouse in Košice with food and used clothing. By chance, Anyu's cousin Alexander Stransky, also a Holocaust survivor, was in charge of the distribution of used American clothing, plus canned food, cigarettes and bananas. As his relatives, we had an edge on selecting the best used clothing for ourselves. I loved climbing the mountain of colorful coats, shirts, pants, jackets, sweaters, blouses, and skirts. Alex would let us in after hours and the three of us would sort through piles of stylish, donated *shmates* (old clothing) from our American co-religionists. We loved wearing their discards. We decided American Jews must have been very rich to give away practically brand new clothing, a true blessing, since we needed many things to keep us warm in the winter.

The first time I tasted canned food, a banana, and American chewing gum was at the end of the war in 1946 at the age of eleven. Apu and Anyu enjoyed American-made cigarettes like Camels, Marlboro and Chesterfields. Slowly we began to recover from the twin tragedies of a devastating World War II and the Holocaust which almost annihilated all of Europe's Jews.

It became clear with each passing day that many of us who survived were damaged human beings, fearful and emotionally shattered. By moving to Israel, I hoped I could repair my faith in humanity, leave fear behind, and walk the streets with pride and dignity, not having to breath the air contaminated by evil hatred and curses. This is why I was shocked when I learned that the adults in my family considered immigrating to South America instead. They wanted to leave, but only to live once again among non-Jews, which made no sense to me. Those countries didn't want Jews to move there! We would have to falsify our birth certificates again to legally apply for visas. What was the matter with my family? Had they lost their pride? God had given us a land of our own.

"Why would any reasonable thinking Jew want to live somewhere else?" I argued. "If you want to go to Venezuela, you'll have to go without me. Take my sister, but I am going to Israel with or without your permission."

Tension erupted among us. My Uncles Jeno and Adolf soon changed their minds, deciding again to go to Israel. Apu's brothers Arnošť and Teodor had no intention of leaving Czechoslovakia. They were perfectly satisfied to live in the new regime. Arnošť, a menswear salesman, had been promoted to management, and Teodor was studying at the University in Prague to become a physician. Cousin Alex Stransky and his family were planning to leave for Israel. So far only the Zingers, Aunt Ella and Uncle Moric and their daughters with their new spouses had left for South America.

To acquire the necessary papers for immigration to Israel was a lengthy process but we began in earnest. The Communist authorities were difficult and corrupt, personally profiting from the departing Jews. My parents began making arrangements to ship furniture and other home accessories and furnishings that they did not want to leave behind. This required the purchase of a "lift," a specially manufactured wooden shipping container to withstand the transport of heavy contents. Due to increased demand, it took three to four months for the manufacturer to produce one. Further, to obtain passage on a ship from nearby Romania to Israel meant entering our name on a long waiting list. All this had been put into motion by my parents and uncle Jeno. We planned to travel together.

The earliest departure would be late spring, by May or June 1949. I had by then become a proud member of the Israel *aliya* group in my B'nai Akiva chapter. Most of my friends' families were leaving or planned to leave for Israel. Spirits were high. We continued our education in Hebrew trying to learn basic expressions so when we arrived we wouldn't feel like total strangers. Time moved slowly. My parents purchased U.S. dollars on the black market, the preferred currency for immigration and, although excited, we all felt some hesitation. After all, it was not so easy to leave your country of birth and start life over from scratch, and my parents often questioned their decision, admitting moments of despair.

In my view, once again, the trip looked like a grand adventure. To me, Israelis were heroes and I wanted to become one of them. They knew how to fight their enemies, not live in fear like we did here. I wanted to be able to pray freely and celebrate my holidays along with everyone else.

Obtaining all the government permits was a big headache. Of course, a fee was attached to every official form and corruption was rampant. It helped to have connections. So many people were leaving for Israel that even getting train reservations via the Zionist organization in charge of scheduling departures to the Romanian port of Constanta was difficult. Trains were booked through the end of April. All the delays made me very nervous and impatient. I wanted out, worried my parents might change their minds. With every hurdle they got discouraged. Finally, a letter arrived confirming our departure during the first week in May!

The letter was a crucial document for securing the exit visa. Everything started to move. I began counting the days to our departure. The news from Israel meanwhile was good; fighting had come to a halt and a cease-fire had been established. Thousands of new *olim* (immigrants) began pouring in. When I went to the movie theater, the Kino, I was excited to see the world news reports on "Movietone" because they always showed a segment about Israel. Over time, they also showed propaganda from the USSR consisting of major achievements by Russian factories. In the early years of WWII, the movie screen was filled with footage of Hitler. Now it was filled with the fatherly image of Josef Stalin. While Hitler scared me, Stalin calmed me down. But there were no more Walt Disney cartoons. Now Apu and I watched Russian-made films on war-related stories in black and white, all very sad or serious.

Our apartment began emptying out as we filled up the container with furniture and household items to be shipped to Israel about a month before we boarded the train. We had approximately one week before the customs officers came to inspect the contents and seal the door in time for the shipping company to pick it up. The list of prohibited items was quite long. Jewels, precious metals, collectibles and art were based on weight and value.

Some inspectors were easier than others. The corrupt ones expected to be paid off, others checked the contents extensively. Others asked questions, and based on the answers, decided how to proceed. People who lied faced stiff fines and penalties and unpleasant consequences, sometimes cancellation of exit permits, or even jail time. In spite of all this, Anyu and Apu asked me to help conceal a couple of valuable religious objects inside the furniture. They felt sure I would know how.

Naturally, we endured some tense moments at inspection until the shipment was finally approved and the lift was officially sealed for shipping. With the apartment empty, reality set in. By this time, I had turned 14 and could hardly wait for my birthday present – our move to Israel. We would have to celebrate Passover here in Košice. but it was not clear where the Seders would be held. Besides, since the end of the war, holidays had become very sad occasions. We didn't even know if the Communist government would allow the baking of matzos, the required unleavened bread. It made no difference to me. Mentally, I was not even there anymore. In school I daydreamed, trying to envision our new life. My grades suffered. With our emigration came a new type of prejudice. We were called traitors by some hot-headed Communists. Many were happy to see us leave. As the day of our departure neared, we had to say goodbye to friends and acquaintances. The Šolc family, our heroes and saviors back in Prešov would be missed most of all.

Boarding the train to Bratislava, was a surreal experience. We had five suitcases and a few more bags. Porters helped us load the baggage. A few more Jewish families also boarded with large, heavy suitcases. A representative from the *Sochnut*, the Jewish Agency in Israel, helped with the departure. The whole process was a spectacle curiously observed by the other passengers.

In Bratislava, we transferred to another train with assigned cars and compartments reserved for departing immigrants for Israel. Sochnut agents collaborated with the Slovak immigration authorities in processing several hundred passengers with luggage and anyone who needed assistance. The scene was chaotic with people pushing and shoving, trying to get ahead in the long lines. Permission was finally given to board. Travelers had their favorite sides and seats and were in a hurry to occupy them. Arguments and disagreements followed, many quite heated and vulgar. In a couple of cars down the track, two men got into a physical altercation. The conductor threatened to remove them from the train. The four of us ended up sitting in the end compartment of the car near the toilet and exit doors. Uncle Jeno and Aunt Terez sat in the car next to ours. We finally left Bratislava in the late afternoon and the chatter of wheels calmed everyone down. Within an hour or so, a relaxed and friendly atmosphere replaced the frenzied beginning of our trip. Conversations ensued among strangers while children befriended other children and played in the aisles. Pajamas and slippers came out of suitcases and carry-on bags, followed by sandwiches, assorted foods, fruits, fragrant hard-boiled eggs and beverages, cold and warm. Rolls of salami, fried chicken, chopped liver salads and potato salads appeared, plus milk for the children and all kinds of candies. Soon the car smelled like a rolling kosher restaurant.

Religious services *mincha* and *maariv* (traditional afternoon and evening services) started just before sundown and ended after sunset. Pious men lined up in the car's corridor and prayed with the same fervor as in their synagogues. In one service, we were supposed to face east, standing up at attention, the heels of our shoes touching. That was tricky on a moving train, which kept zig-zagging and changing directions. Someone ruled that we all start praying together at the moment the train headed eastward, and not to worry about turns. "Just keep *davening* (praying)." The wonderful thing about our religion is the ability to adjust our worship and practices to the prevailing conditions. Logic and reason must replace the rigidity of Biblical laws. God is everywhere, therefore, we may pray anywhere.

For three days and nights we became a synagogue on wheels. Not everyone on this train was Orthodox, but we were all Jews, speeding to reach our Holy Land, coping with discomfort, even with some insults from border guards and other uniformed officials as we traveled through Hungary and Romania. The train made a few stops in the middle of nowhere. The first night the train stopped in Budapest for several hours. No one ever told us why or for what purpose. During one of the following stops in a small town in Hungary, inspectors boarded, checking the passengers' travel documents. The same thing happened in Romania.

Once, upon stopping, a family was removed from the train by border patrol agents. Another time a sick passenger was taken off the train and rushed to a hospital. Exhausted from lack of sleep and constant confinement, we counted the hours before our arrival in Constanta. Our family's most nerve-wracking moment occurred between Bratislava and Budapest. During random inspections, Slovak customs agents checked passengers for illegal valuables such as American dollars or excessive amounts of gold jewelry and diamonds. Passengers breaking the strict laws by concealing or smuggling valuables over the permitted value stood the chance of having them confiscated by the agents and worse. If the violation was extensive, the violators were removed from the train and sent back to Bratislava's court of law.

One of the inspectors walked by our compartment, then turned back and asked various questions as to what we had in our possession such as jewels, watches, foreign currency, etc. He searched our suitcases and asked Apu to empty his suit jacket and trousers pockets. He asked Anyu to empty her handbag. And as a final request, he ordered all of us to remove our shoes. At this point Anyu started to charm him with small talk. This was her method to overcome fear and eminent danger. I became tense and somewhat worried when she started removing her shoes. Two days before our departure from Košice, Anyu was desperate to find a way to take her beautiful diamond ring with her to Israel. I came up with an idea "Anyuka, if you let me, I will hide your ring in one of your high-heel shoes." After some doubt, she agreed. However, the diamond had to be removed from its setting in order for to me to drill a hole into the heel and sink the stone into it. I enjoyed the challenge and Anyu was pleased with the quality of my work. I was proud of my inventiveness. But when I watched Anyu remove her left shoe, I got terribly scared. I thought if he'd ever found a hidden object in a heel, he would have known how to look for it. I prayed silently, "*Pán Božko drahy,* don't let him investigate the left shoe."

He put his hand into the right shoe, pushing around with his fingers. Then the left shoe, he looked into it, turned it over, shook it and gave it back to Anyu. As he walked away, a terrible weight fell off my shoulders. I looked at Anyu and Apu, wanting to see their reaction to what just happened. Anyu stepped back into her shoes and a big smile appeared on her face. When we all sat down, she gave me a

big hug and a kiss. Fortunately, the inspector also failed to find the
U.S. dollars that Apu had put aside, essential for our arrival in our
new homeland.

On the third day, we arrived in Constanta in Romania. The four
cars filled with immigrants were disconnected from the rest of the
train which was left parked at the entrance to the harbor. We were
told that since we arrived late in the day, we would have to spend
the night in the cars. We were allowed to get off and catch a breath
of fresh air and replenish our drinking water with a warning not to
leave the immediate surroundings. Everyone was filled with anticipation of sailing on the ship anchored before us. High spirits domi-
nated the last night on the train. I walked through all the cars, visiting my aunt and uncle and a few other people I recognized from our
Eastern Slovakian region. We were now under Romanian jurisdiction, no longer threatened by corrupt Communist inspectors from
Slovakia and Hungary. The Romanian government provided armed
security guards to protect our safety on and around the railway cars
and inside the harbor until our departure on board the steamship.

A couple of representatives from the Sochnut were responsible
for our well-being on our voyage and safe arrival in Haifa. The night
consisted of spirited conversations, parties and very little sleep. The
morning started with the transfer of luggage to the harbor authority building. Long lines formed for processing exit papers and issu-
ing ship boarding permits. The long, tedious process lasted several
hours until finally, we were able to board the ship in the afternoon.
Crammed into the hull, we settled into narrow rows of army cots.
Two additional levels rose above the hull, occupied by non-emigrant
passengers in individual cabins. This ship was originally built for
handling cargo and some passengers. It now had human beings as

its total cargo. As a result, it had inadequate numbers of toilets and a shortage of water therefore drinking water was rationed. No one was allowed to leave the bottom level without permission from the crewmembers assigned to our sleeping area.

Soon after the ship sailed into the open waters of the Black Sea the hull began to creak. This was my first time on a ship and I didn't like the noises around me. On top of that, I was a poor swimmer. I was panic-stricken, worried about the vessel's integrity. *Were we going to be dumped into the sea due to excessive load?* Of course, I kept these thoughts to myself. The fear was mine to deal with. Not long after we left the Constanta harbor the sun started to set only adding to my misery.

As people retired for the night and conversations ceased, the creaking sounds lessened but I couldn't fall asleep. I felt trapped. When I finally fell asleep from exhaustion, I was awakened by commotion, some early morning excitement. The word had spread quickly that our ship had entered the Bosporus Strait and soon we would be sailing along the shores of the splendid city of Istanbul. Curiosity created a mob scene, and our guards became helpless, unable to hold back the crowd from ascending the steps to the upper decks.

A splendid view of the palaces and the minarets of Istanbul suddenly appeared to our left. The great number of people pushing forward to the rails on one side of the ship created a tipping sensation. Within minutes, the captain ordered us to spread out on the deck to avoid the ship from listing too far to the left. As we were sliding along the edge of the city, a light fog lifted, reflecting the sun's rays. The whole experience was dream-like and surreal. The Bosporus Strait was a busy and noisy body of water with no apparent rules of navigation. Sea-going vessels of various sizes and colors plowed the waters, fast and furious towards their destinations. Getting out of the ship's belly for the view was quite a welcome relief, even though it did not last long. We were ordered to return to the lower level and stay there for the rest of the voyage.

But the next day my curiosity drove me to explore the upper decks of our ship anyway. My keen senses were handy features when one wanted to sneak around and avoid capture. After dark or early morning presented the best opportunities to stay undetected. I enjoyed inhaling the fresh salty air on the top deck, surely superior to the air we breathed down below. I would find a hidden corner and render myself invisible until sunrise. The Mediterranean Sea was smooth and shiny like a mirror reflecting the light of the moon. I eagerly counted the remaining hours, imagining our arrival to the harbor. Anyu and Apu warned me about the danger of slipping and falling overboard, but I told them that I was not alone sneaking around. A few other kids my age were also exploring other parts of the ship.

Aunt Ružena, cousin Turko, myself and my mother, c. 1940

Ružena Jung, Moshe Grünfeld, and my mother, c. 1937

CHAPTER 44

Arriving in Israel
May 1949

The closer we came to our destination the more impatient everyone became. The ship's crew basically lost control over the restless kids and so did their parents. A festive mood had overtaken the entire ship. On the last day someone ran down and yelled, "Land of Israel on the horizon!" which prompted an unstoppable stampede to the upper deck. At first sight it looked like a mirage, hazy outlines appearing and disappearing into the mist. Within an hour, the coastline became sharp and visible. We were definitely approaching land.

The captain of the ship confirmed over the loudspeaker that we were northwest of Israel's shore, approximately four to five hours from Haifa. The announcement triggered jubilation. The young people began singing and dancing the *hora,* a folk dance in a circle, to the accompaniment of several musicians, led by the Israeli staff on board. The last few hours I was glued to the railing, focused on the scenery. The shoreline appeared to be mostly sand and rock with occasional clusters of houses and palm trees, plus steep hills rising above a large bay. Many houses and buildings covered the highest hill facing the water. Someone excitedly exclaimed, "That's Mount Carmel. We are almost in Haifa!"

Families embraced as the ship, assisted by a tugboat, slowly approached the entrance to the harbor. Anyu, Apu, little Marika and I hugged and kissed, laughed and cried. Our joy and elation, mixed with a certain degree of apprehension about the unknown future and the new beginning, is truly hard to describe. The festivities and the celebration were sustained mostly by the young Zionists, mostly in their early twenties, joined by adolescents my age and slightly older. Unfortunately, most of the younger children died in the camps, murdered by the Nazis.

Most everybody returned to the hull and started carrying suitcases and bags upstairs in anticipation of disembarkation. Instead, there was a long wait and confusion. The Sochnut agents left the ship, picked up by harbor shuttle, and the ship's crew had no information whatsoever. Several hours had passed by the time an agent returned to share the disappointing news. The harbor authorities had closed early to celebrate the first Israel Independence Day. That meant that we had to spend another night on the ship and most likely, most of the next day as well.

There was only one thing left to do. Join in with the Israeli population and celebrate the very first birthday of our new homeland. Following dinner, the dancing began and went on and on and on, non-stop, until the wee hours of the morning on May 14, 1949. I could hardly believe it. Israel and freedom were within our reach. After all we had been through, my dreams had been realized.

Sgt. Oscar Sladek / Israel Defense Forces.
Composer & accompanist of the Lahakat Pikud Tzafon,
the performing arts troupe of the Northern Command, c. 1955

Singer/songwriter Oscar Sladek, c. 1960
Photo: Jack Goldman

Prešov, Slovakia - 2022
Photo: Peter Dobrovský
www.PeterDobrovsky.sk

Summer, 2006
The building I'm seated in front of in Liptovsky Svaty Mikulas
was occupied in May 1944 by German military forces.
This is the very building where I saw barefoot German
soldiers fleeing from when the partisans attacked.

From the desk of

OSCAR SLADEK

March 1, 2022

The survival of my family could have never taken place without the help of Judge Jozef Šolc, a righteous Christian, and his wife Margita. With his help, my parents chose to become fugitives from a despotic Fascist government rather than follow a law-abiding Jewish community to its tragic end. In 2006, I returned to Prešov and made a visit to the cemetery where I found their graves and bade my final respects. Jozef will forever rest in my mind as an angel of salvation who stood by us and secured our safety during the darkest hours.

From left to right; Dr. Jozef Šolc, his mother Mária Šolcová (sitting in the armchair), his sister Mária Šolcová, his wife Margita Šolcová, and seated at the bottom are the two children Samuel Šolc and Emília Šolcová . This picture was taken on Christmas eve 1943 in Prešov. Photo courtesy of Family of Dr. Jozef Šolc.

Further, I have to acknowledge my courageous, creative and relentless mother who never gave up and found a way through every situation, no matter what. Her courage and ingenuity inspire me to this day. Both she and my talented father helped me to survive and reach adulthood while countless others perished. They lived on and were part of our lives as we moved from Israel to South America to California and lastly to Denver, Colorado where we settled. I honor their memories and miss them both, wishing they could have met their remarkable grandchildren and great-grandchildren.

Without the help and support of the following individuals, this book would have never come to pass. My deepest gratitude goes to many organizations and their staff members who, during the past 50 years of my life, believed in the educational value of my survival story. Through their efforts, I had hundreds of opportunities to share it with Americans of all ages and backgrounds.

With very special thanks to the Anti-Defamation League of Colorado and Susan Parker Gerson, Program Coordinator for ADL's "Words to Action", and to the Arapahoe County Library System and Jan Alekseiewicz, Senior Events Specialist, and to Colorado Military Installations, Captain Anne Green. Thanks to the Colorado Agency for Jewish Education and Israel Study Tour, and former Director and Teen Outreach coordinator, Josh Samet.

To all The Denver Public Library branch locations and to the Intermountain Jewish News, including its award-winning journalists Larry Hankin, Andrea Jacobs, and Chris Leppek, plus publisher Rabbi Hillel Goldberg. To Denver's Mizel Museum and especially Penny Nisson, Education Director and staff member, Jan Nadav. To Congregation Temple Emanuel education director Ron Leff who invited me to speak to all pre-confirmation students, and especially to Rabbi Raymond A. Zwerin, Emeritus, founding rabbi of Temple Sinai in Denver who encouraged me to begin sharing my personal survival story during his annual confirmation class retreats while I served as the Congregation's Executive Director. And to Rabbi Rick Rheins, senior rabbi at Temple Sinai, who over the last decade has invited me every year to sing *Zog Mir Keynmol*, the Warsaw ghetto Partisans Song, at the start of Yom Kippur *Yizkor services* (a memorial service held by Jewish people on certain holy days for deceased relatives or martyrs).

Thanks also to Dr. Sarah Pessin, former executive director of the Holocaust Awareness Institute at the University of Denver and to Selena Neumoff, HAI Speaker's Bureau Director.

Very special thanks are due to Wayne Armstrong, official photographer for the University of Denver, who was responsible for creating all the outstanding Holocaust survivors' photographs for the permanent exhibition titled "Abide" at the Mizel Museum in Denver. This exhibit features survivors who made Denver their home after the Shoah. Also to Tracy Wells for your help, and to photographers Peter Dobrovsky and Ivan Kmit for contributing your beautiful scenic photography of Slovakia, as noted.

To my children, I could not have done any of this without your collective support and encouragement. Thank you to my eldest son Ron and his daughter Sara who helped make the original transcription from my handwritten notebooks and historical guidance; and to my youngest son Michael and daughter Adena for your creative and editorial input, and to my *gantse macher* son Daniel who brough his own skills and dedication to further spearhead the publishing of this work. The end result of this collective effort is the book you now read.

Sincere thanks also to Corinne Joy Brown, accomplished writer, longtime friend, collaborator and book shepherd who helped bring this story to life. With appreciation for her patience, sensitivity and talent. Special thanks also to Chris Taaffe for helping launch this book and to Linda Katchen, for her editorial assistance. Appreciation is also extended to

Tore Schulman, interviewer, and Abby Rosenblum, segment producer of *"The Daily Blast"*, KUSA Channel 9 (NBC), Colorado, to Sharon Levy, and to Michael Hughes and Ryan Warner at Colorado Public Radio for your support. Appreciation to James Carroll, Ambassador Akbar Ahmed, Beth Kean, David Patterson, Rabbi Jay Strear, Scott Levin, Rabbi Rick Rheins, Penny Nisson, Andy Mallen, David Permut and Chris Leppek for your 'first reads' and providing encouraging advance critical praise of this memoir.

If it were not for my dear parents' deep love and caring, and their dedication to my safety, I might not have survived the Shoah. And without the Zinger family's willingness to open their home to me, exposing a rich, cultural experience, this story might have had a very different ending.

Most important, I could not have lived this fulfilling life complete with music, comfort, family, delicious meals and the richness of our Jewish traditions without my beautiful wife of 63 years, Selma Rosen Sladek, whose love and companionship has made my life so worthwhile (and whose determination and support of this memoir is unquestionably appreciated). Selma has been by my side at nearly every speaking engagement, giving me encouragement and making sure my presentation was complete. Thanks to her, I am the father of four amazing human beings: our three sons Ron, Daniel, and Michael, and our beautiful daughter Adena, all adults living with their wonderful families in the USA.

To my loving family, and my extended family (including my sister Mimi, Uncle Tidi, cousins Gaby, Dany, Turko, Stefko, Judy, Roszi and your families), one and all, *thank you* for encouraging me to share my story with the world.

It is important to acknowledge that my family was deeply grounded in our religion, in the observance and tenets of our faith, and the belief in an all-powerful God that has been the source of strength for the Jewish people for thousands of years. That belief has played a major role in our family's survival.

Selma and Oscar Sladek
Denver, Colorado 2019

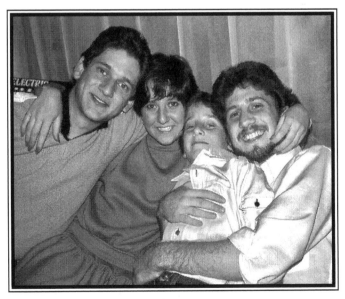

Daniel, Adena, Michael, Ron
This photo reflects the contentment and happiness Selma and I achieved with
the creation of a wonderful loving family. I didn't want my children to be
burdened with my difficult past, but to live free and happy lives.

Bedrich 'Frici', Sarlota 'Irene', Oskar 'Osi' and Miriam 'Mimi' Sladek
Caracas, Venezuela late 1950s

In memory of my beloved parents
who risked everything that I might survive.

A Letter from Osi's Sister Miriam (Mimi) Miller

As Osi Sladek's much younger sister, I was fortunate enough to have missed entirely the horrific events my family went thru. Osi was thirteen years older than me, therefore I sometimes felt like I had three parents. That said, they all spoiled me equally, protecting me from harm and danger. My mother indulged me, a second child she long awaited.

Neither my mother or my father spoke about the roundups and persecutions of Jews in Slovakia, and their flight into the countryside under a false identity, or the hardships of hiding in the mountains in bitter cold, but occasionally, as I grew up, I found her weeping. She told me she was crying for her mother who was murdered in the Shoah. That feeling of loss never left her.

Even after I matured and left home, I remember one thing in particular my mother always said to me and Osi. "Whatever or whomever you're dealing with, deal with them so you can face them again with dignity." As a result, I grew up wanting a life free from conflict, always seeking ways to keep the peace.

Our mother passed at the age of 53. My father at 69. I married at 19 and regret that my mother never met my husband or children. But my brother and I faced the world with unwavering confidence and enough skills to adapt to any situation. As a result of all the languages we spoke, a result of many attempts at resettlement, I became a professional interpreter and translator, a great gift around which I built a career in Canada. Osi became a fluid performer in many languages, touching the hearts of people all over the world. I share this bond with him, a special legacy to the circumstances of his childhood and mine. On this occasion, I applaud the courage it took to recount his remarkable story and admire to this day the little boy who braved fear and deprivation to come through it all intact.

> To the brother I love and admire,
> Miriam "Mimi" Miller
> Toronto, Canada

OSCAR SLADEK

Photo: Wayne Armstrong

Over the past six decades, Oscar 'Osi' Sladek has been regarded as a dedicated and respected professional and cultural / educational leader in Colorado's Jewish community. His positive impact has been considerable. Oscar is a child survivor of the Holocaust from Presov, Czechoslovakia, (now Slovakia) who immigrated to the United States in the late 1950s and settled in Colorado in 1960 with his wife Selma Rosen Sladek. They have four children, seven grandchildren and two great-grandchildren.

He is an accomplished composer, musician and singer. After WWII, he emerged as a popular folk artist in Israel where he served in the Israel Defense Forces for three years as musical director and composer of the Northern Command Enter-tainment Corps. Thereafter, Sladek was a performer on the folk music scene in Hollywood, CA during the late 1950's. In addition to his solo performances, he appeared alongside Rachel Hadass and Theodore Bikel. He and Selma met there, fell in love and moved to Denver where Oscar continued performing. Notably, he headlined the 1960 Colorado Folk Festival at the Denver Auditorium Arena, shar-ing the stage with Judy Collins, Odetta, Josh White, and other legendary singers.

Since that time, Oscar has dedicated his life to Holocaust awareness and educa-tion, having been one of the first (and youngest) survivors in Colorado to publicly speak about his life. Osi continues to be one of the state's most prolific speakers, addressing thousands of children and adults of all backgrounds - in schools, prisons, multi-faith organizations, military bases, universities, libraries, government offices and more. His musical performances and public speaking engagements have continued over the past sixty years throughout the Rocky Mountains Region, Toronto (Canada) and Southern California. He has also provided steadfast guidance as a community leader who spent the bulk of his career working as executive director of Jewish non-profit organizations.

In 2019, Governor Jared Polis presented Osi Sladek with an award honoring his "commitment to inspire understanding, moral courage and social responsibility" at the Mizel Annual Dinner, one of Colorado's largest philanthropic events.

Colorado Governor Jared Polis presents an award to Holocaust survivor
Oscar 'Osi' Sladek at the 2019 Mizel Institute Annual Dinner.
A well-known folk singer, songwriter, Jewish community leader and now, author,
Sladek was honored for his 'commitment to inspire understanding,
moral courage and social responsibility'.
Photo: Mizel Institute

Oscar Sladek, Holocaust survivor, shares his story with Airmen
during the Days of Remembrance event at Schriever Air Force Base, Colorado.
As a young boy, Sladek spent several years evading capture by Nazis. His story served as
a reminder of the persecution and difficulties people faced during the Holocaust.
U.S. Air Force photos by Kathryn Calvert

Štaub Family Members Who Perished in the Shoah

Maria Degner (married name Ziegler, sister of Helene)

Helene "Linka" Degner (married name Bein, sister of Maria)

Jakub Štaub (married to Henrietta)

Henrietta Ziegler (daughter of Maria Degner, married to Jakub Štaub)

Viliam Jung (married to Ružena Štaub)

Josephine (Pepi) Friedman

Teri Friedman (mother was Josephine)

Grünfeld Family Members Who Perished in the Shoah

Hermina Shuh (married name Grünfeld)

Soli Grünfeld (married to Berta)

Berta Grünfeld (married to Soli)

Jossi Grünfeld (son of Soli and Berta)

Child Grünfeld (daughter of Soli and Berta)

Pityu (Pinchas) Grünfeld (married to Ilonka)

Ilonka Grünfeld (married to Pinchas)

Jossi Grünfeld (son of Pinchas and Ilonka)

Child Grünfeld (daughter of Pinchas and Ilonka)

Málschi (Malka) Grünfeld (married to Blaustein; married again to Gross)

Husband Gross (married to Málschi)

Jolanka Gross (daughter of Málschi and Husband)

Rōzsi Grünfeld (married name Birnbaum, wife of Armin)

Armin Birnbaum (married to Ružena)

Osi Birnbaum (son of Ružena and Armin)

Agi Birnbaum (daughter of Ružena and Armin)

Manci Grünfeld (married to Abraham "Adolf")

Ervin Grünfeld (son of Abraham and Manci)

Vera Grünfeld (daughter of Abraham and Manci)

Irenka Grünfeld (daughter of Jakub "Jeno" and Terez)

Agi Grünfeld (daughter of Jakub "Jeno" and Terez)

CORINNE JOY BROWN

Photo: E.J. Carr

As a journalist, Corinne freelances for a variety of print publications, including "Cowboys & Indians", "Western Art & Architecture", "Colorado Life", "Home & Garden Colorado" and others. She was formerly a staff writer for "Working Ranch" magazine, "True West" and "Persimmon Hill", the publication of the National Cowboy and Western Heritage Museum in Oklahoma.

Since, 2015, Corinne has been editor-in chief of "HaLapid," the publication of the Society for Crypto-Judaic Studies, a secular, academic organization committed to the study of the forcefully converted Iberian Jews of the Middle Ages and their global descendants. As a multi-award winning, published author, she is currently working on her ninth book. She looks forward to the release of the sequel to her first novel, "MacGregor's Lantern," titled "MacGregor's Return" in 2022.

Corinne is a professional member and past president of the Denver Woman's Press Club and a founding member of Women Writing the West. She is a member of Western Writers of America and the Colorado Independent Publishers Association. Corinne was named a Fellow of the University of Colorado History Dept in 2014. She is an alumna of Boston University's School of Fine and Applied Arts and has a graduate degree in design from the Interior Design Institute. She was the original founder of Writing the West, a 20 year accredited writing program held at Western State College in Gunnison, Colorado.

Corinne and her husband own a home furnishings gallery founded in 1976 (Zoli Contemporary Living) and are importers of European high-end home furnishings. Corinne is an Allied Member of the American Society of Interior Designers. When not writing, she spends her free time designing jewelry and playing with their German Shepherd.

Other books by Corinne Joy Brown

Awesome Art For Horse-Lovin' Kids

Come and Get It: The Saga of Western Dinnerware

Finding Home

Hidden Star

MacGregor's Lantern

Sanctuary Ranch

Why Not Them?

Wishful Watoosi

www.corinnejoybrown.com

In memory of the six million Jewish human beings
who were systematically murdered at the hands of the Nazis, simply for being Jewish.
These photos were taken at the Auschwitz-Birkenau concentration camp rail siding,
as innocent men, women and children head for the gas chambers and crematoriums.
Photo: United States Holocaust Memorial Museum, courtesy of Yad Vashem

These Jewish brothers, Israel and Zelig Jacob,
ages 9 and 11, were murdered at Auschwitz. They were children
just like me who were captured by the Nazis and their collaborators.
Photo: United States Holocaust Memorial Museum, courtesy of Yad Vashem

Made in the USA
Columbia, SC
06 August 2022